KAPLAN

K12 LEARNING SERVICES

Kaplan

ADVANTAGE

New York

Mathematics

GRADE

3

Kaplan Advantage
New York Mathematics Grade 3

TOC

Table of Contents

Student Introduction

Welcome to Kaplan Advantage

The New York State Math Test

Hello and welcome! Chances are you have already heard something about the New York State Math Test. One of the best ways to prepare for a test is to learn about the test itself. So let's get started by seeing what you already know about the test.

What Do You Already Know?

Read each statement below. Use what you know about the Math Test to determine whether the statement is correct and circle either True or False to show your answer.

1. You can use a calculator on the New York State Math Test.

    True   False

2. All questions on the New York State Math Test are multiple choice.

    True   False

3. Not all the questions on the test will be worth the same number of points.

    True   False

4. You will take the test over two days.

    True   False

5. There is no way to know what will be on the test.

    True   False

Were You Correct?

1. You can use a calculator on the New York State Math Test.

FALSE: You cannot use a calculator for any part of the test. You will need to be able to add, subtract, multiply, and divide using a pencil and paper or using mental math.

2. All questions on the New York State Math Test are multiple choice.

FALSE: In addition to multiple-choice questions, there are also open-ended questions for which you will write out your answer. You will earn points for getting the answer right, but you will also earn points for showing your work and explaining your thinking.

3. Not all the questions on the test will be worth the same number of points.

TRUE: Multiple-choice questions on the test are worth one point. Some open-ended questions are worth two points. Others are worth three points.

4. You will take the test over two days.

TRUE: On the first day, you will complete Book 1. All the questions will be multiple choice. On the second day, you will answer open-ended questions in Book 2.

5. There is no way to know what will be on the test.

FALSE: Although you can't know exactly what each question will be about, you *can* know what the test writers consider a fair topic and an unfair topic. The test will cover the math you have learned in school through April of this year.

About the Grade 3 Math Test

The Math Test is given in two sessions over two days. Here is what you can expect to happen each day.

Book	Number of Multiple-Choice Questions	Number of Short-Response Questions	Number of Extended-Response Questions	Testing Time
1	40	0	0	60 minutes
2	0	4	2	40 minutes
Total	40	4	2	100 minutes

On the first day of the test, you will be asked to answer only **multiple-choice** questions. These questions each have four possible answer choices. Only one answer choice will be right. You must find the correct answer. Each multiple-choice question is worth one point.

On the second day of the test, you will be asked to answer **open-ended** questions. These questions do not have any possible choices listed. You must find the answer and show your work. Sometimes, you will also need to explain your thinking. Short-response questions are worth two points. Extended-response questions are worth three points. Extended-response questions usually take longer to solve and have more parts.

How to Use This Book

15 Lessons to Learn the Strategies

Each lesson has four parts.

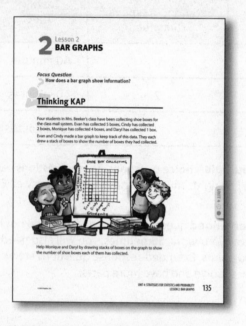

In the Thinking KAP, you will solve a real-world problem about math you learned last year.

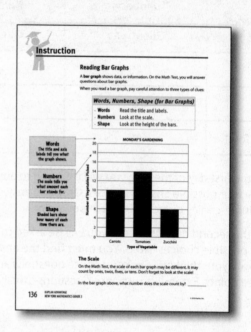

In the Instruction, you will learn new strategies and review important concepts.

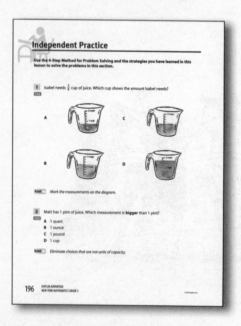

In the Independent Practice, you will use the strategies you have learned to answer test-like questions.

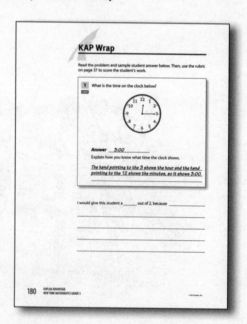

In the KAP Wrap, you will score a sample student response to an open-ended test question.

3 Mini Practice Tests and a Full-Length Practice Test to Practice Strategies

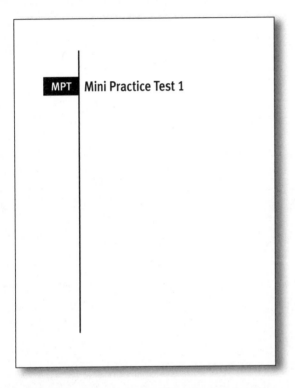

Throughout the program, you will also practice using the strategies you have learned by taking Mini Practice Tests and a Full-Length Practice Test. The Full-Length Practice Test appears at the end of the program. Three Mini Practice Tests appear throughout the book.

After each Mini Practice Test, and after the Full-Length Practice Test, you will complete a Reflection. This is your chance to record your thoughts about how easy or difficult each question was for you, and which strategy helped you the most.

Extra Practice for Every Performance Indicator

After the Full-Length Practice Test, you will find extra practice for every performance indicator that might appear on the test. If you find a topic difficult, you can use this section to build your skills.

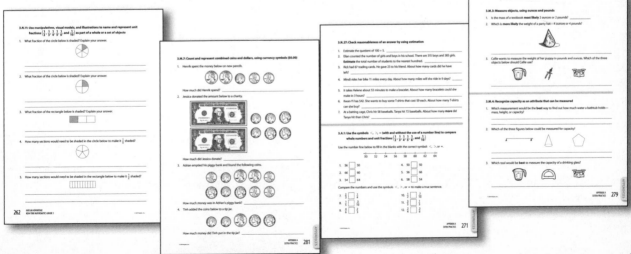

UNIT 1 | The 4-Step Method for Problem Solving

I USE PROBLEM SOLVING TO REPAIR COMPUTERS.

COMPUTER TECHNICIAN

1 Lesson 1
GETTING READY

Focus Question
How can you better understand problems before you solve them?

Thinking KAP

Solve both problems below.

1. $893 - 354 = ?$

    Answer _____

2. To climb to the top of the Washington Monument, you have to go up 893 stairs. To get to the top of the Statue of Liberty, you have to climb 354 stairs. How many **more** stairs are there at the Washington Monument than the Statue of Liberty?

    Answer _____ stairs

What do you notice about problems 1 and 2?

_____

_____

_____

Which problem was more difficult to solve?

_____

_____

_____

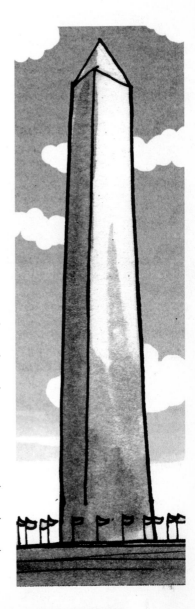

Instruction

Getting Started

Welcome to *Kaplan Advantage*! In each lesson of this program, you will learn strategies for solving problems. The best place to start is by learning a method that can help you with any problem—the 4-Step Method for Problem Solving.

Many of the problems on the Math Test will be word problems. The 4-Step Method for Problem Solving will help you understand and work through word problems, so you can solve them more easily.

The 4-Step Method for Problem Solving

1 Step 1: Understand the problem.

2 Step 2: Analyze important information.

3 Step 3: Plan and solve.

4 Step 4: Check your work.

How is the 4-Step Method for Problem Solving like methods you have used before? How is it different?

_____

_____

_____

_____

Understanding the Problem

Before you solve a math problem, you need to figure out what the problem is basically about and what you are being asked to find.

---

1 **Step 1:** Understand the problem.

- Scan the problem.
- Restate the question in your own words.

Scan the Problem

When you see a math problem, the first thing you should do is read it once through quickly. As you read, try to get a general sense of what the problem is about. How is this problem like others you have solved before? How is it different?

Restate the Question in Your Own Words

To make sure you understand the problem you are being asked to solve, restate the question in your own words.

▌TRY IT OUT▐▶ **Complete Step 1 for the problem below.**

1
3.N.22
Lisa needs to read 12 books this summer. She has 3 months to finish her reading. How many books should Lisa read each month?

A ▭
B ▭
C ▭
D ▭

> The answer choices have been covered up. Don't solve the problem in Step 1!

What is the problem basically about? _____

_____

Restate the problem in your own words. _____

_____

Analyzing the Important Information

In Step 2, you will read the problem again—this time more carefully. As you read, you will underline the clues.

> **2** **Step 2:** Analyze important information.
>
> - Underline the clues.
> - Rewrite the important information in a helpful way.

What is a clue?

A clue tells you about the math in a problem, not the story. Think of a clue as something that could help you solve the problem.

▌TRY IT OUT▐➡ **Underline the clues in the problem. Then, explain three of the clues on the lines provided.**

1
3.N.22 Lisa needs to read 12 books this summer. She has 3 months to finish her reading. How many books should Lisa read each month?

- **A** 3 books
- **B** 4 books
- **C** 6 books
- **D** 12 books

The clue ___12 books___ tells me ___the total number of books Lisa must read___.

The clue ___3 months___ tells me _____

_____.

The clue _____ tells me _____

_____.

Rewriting the Important Information

It can often be helpful to rewrite the important information in a different way than how it is given to you. Rewriting the information in a diagram or chart can often help you better understand the problem.

Draw It

One way to rewrite important information is to draw a simple diagram to help you understand the information you are given. Diagrams are helpful for problems about parts and totals. They are also helpful for many measurement and geometry problems.

Chart It

Another way to organize information is to make a chart. Charts are most helpful for problems that involve changes over time, patterns and relationships, and data from surveys or experiments.

❚TRY IT OUT❚➡ **Make a diagram or chart to rewrite the important information in the problem on page 18.**

Independent Practice

Use the 4-Step Method for Problem Solving to solve the problems in this section.

1

3.N.18

On Thursday, 148 people went to see the school play. On Friday, 213 people went. How many **more** people saw the play on Friday?

A 65

B 75

C 351

D 361

hint ▶ *The clue "more" tells you to compare two numbers.*

2

3.N.25

Samantha wants to estimate the sum of the numbers below.

$$12 + 29 + 31$$

Which sum below will give Samantha the **best** estimate?

A 10 + 20 + 30

B 20 + 20 + 30

C 10 + 30 + 30

D 10 + 30 + 40

hint ▶ *"Estimate" is a clue that tells you to round the numbers.*

3

3.N.16

Which list of numbers contains **only** even numbers?

A 4, 6, 12, 20, 28

B 8, 9, 10, 11, 12

C 6, 10, 15, 20, 24

D 9, 11, 17, 21, 25

hint ▶ *Read through all of the numbers in the answer choices before you make your decision.*

4 What is the shape of the party hat shown below?

`3.G.3`

A cone

B cube

C cylinder

D sphere

hint *How is this shape like others you have seen? Think of the names of other objects with the same shape.*

5 Jean buys 4 bags of apples. Each bag has 7 apples in it. What is the total number of apples Jean buys?

`3.N.19`

A 3 apples

B 11 apples

C 28 apples

D 35 apples

hint *Underline the important clues in this word problem to help you organize your thoughts.*

6 Manuel, Dylan, and Reggie are sharing a bag of candy at lunch. There are 18 pieces of candy in the bag. They each get the same number of pieces. Which expression describes how they shared?

`3.N.24`

A $18 + 3$

B $18 - 3$

C 18×3

D $18 \div 3$

hint *Draw a diagram to help you choose an operation.*

7 Kyle has the school books shown below.

3.N.10

What fraction of Kyle's books are math books?

A $\frac{1}{2}$

B $\frac{1}{3}$

C $\frac{1}{4}$

D $\frac{1}{5}$

> hint ▸ *Draw a fraction bar of the picture and compare it to your answer.*

8 Michelle uses the numbers below in a number game.

3.N.4

5   4   7

What is the **greatest** number Michelle can make with 4 in the tens place?

A 457

B 547

C 745

D 754

> hint ▸ *Underline the clue "4 in the tens place." Use this clue with a place-value chart to find your answer.*

9 What time will it be when $\frac{1}{4}$ of an hour has passed?

3.M.8

A 12:30

B 3:15

C 3:30

D 3:45

hint ▷ *Divide the clock into quarters to find the answer.*

10 Terrence spent $0.68 on 5 pencils. Which group of coins shows exactly how much Terrence spent?

3.M.7

A

B

C

D

hint ▷ *Count up the money in the answer choices. Write the amounts next to the picture to help you.*

KAP Wrap

Ryan solved the problem below. He incorrectly answered (B).

---

1 The graph below shows the number of rainy days for the last four months.

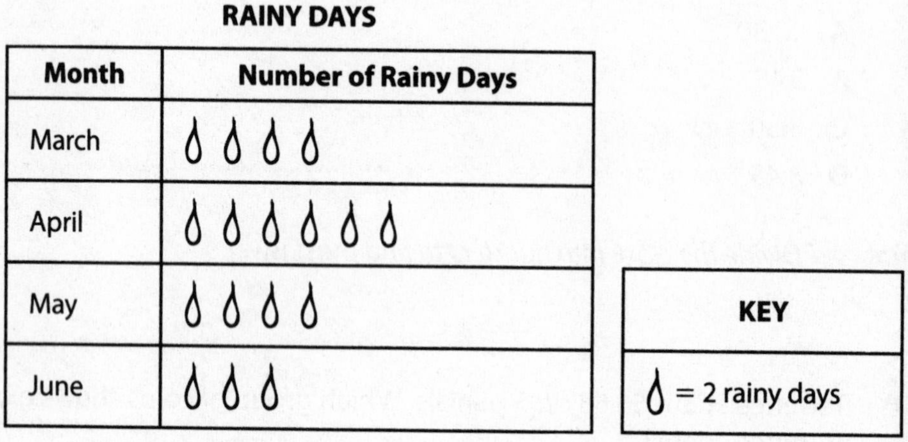

3.S.7

RAINY DAYS

Month	Number of Rainy Days
March	⚬ ⚬ ⚬ ⚬
April	⚬ ⚬ ⚬ ⚬ ⚬ ⚬
May	⚬ ⚬ ⚬ ⚬
June	⚬ ⚬ ⚬

KEY
⚬ = 2 rainy days

In which month were there exactly 6 rainy days?

A March

B April

C May

D June

Describe the error Ryan made. _____

_____

_____

_____

What is the correct answer? _____

2 Lesson 2
TAKING ACTION

Focus Question

What strategies can you use to solve problems and check your work?

Thinking KAP

Underline the important clues in the problem below.

1

3.N.19

Kayla decorates her notebook with 3 rows of stickers. She puts 6 stickers in each row. How many stickers will Kayla use in total?

A 2 stickers

B 3 stickers

C 9 stickers

D 18 stickers

Restate the question in your own words. _____

_____

Make a chart or diagram to analyze the important information.

Instruction

Making a Plan

Once you understand a problem, you need to make a plan to solve it. Look back at what the problem asks for and at the important information you are given. Then, decide how to use what you are given to solve the problem.

3 Step 3: Plan and solve.

- What do you know?
- What do you need?
- How can you use what you know to find what you need?

▌TRY IT OUT▐▶ **Complete Steps 1 and 2 for the problem below. You will solve the problem on the next page.**

1

3.N.25

Alfonzo has 38 yellow balloons, 22 red balloons, and 18 blue balloons for his party on Saturday. What is the **best** estimate of the total number of Alfonzo's balloons?

A 40 balloons

B 60 balloons

C 70 balloons

D 80 balloons

Restate the problem in your own words. _____

_____

Underline the important clues in the problem. Then, draw a diagram or make a chart to help you understand the important information.

❙ TRY IT OUT ❙ → **Now, use the three planning questions from Step 3 to solve the problem on the previous page.**

What do you know?

What information is in the problem? _____

_____

_____

What do you need?

What do you need to find in order to solve the problem? _____

_____

_____

How can you use what you know to find what you need?

Describe your plan.

_____

_____

_____

Carry out your plan to solve the problem.

Checking Your Work

The best way to improve your score on any test is to check your work. To check your work, ask yourself the three questions below.

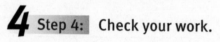

4 Step 4: Check your work.

- Did you answer the right question?
- Is your answer reasonable?
- Can you solve the problem another way?

Did you answer the right question?

One reason students get problems wrong is that they do not answer what the question asks. After you solve a problem, go back to Step 1 and review your restated problem. Is that what you answered?

❚ TRY IT OUT ❚➡ **A student incorrectly solved the problem below. Find the mistake.**

1

3.N.25

Alfonzo has 38 yellow balloons, 22 red balloons, and 18 blue balloons for his party on Saturday. What is the **best** estimate of the total number of Alfonzo's balloons?

    A 40 balloons

    B 60 balloons

    C 70 balloons

    D 80 balloons

Refer to your calculations from the previous page. What mistake could this student have made to get (C) as an answer?

_____

_____

_____

Is your answer reasonable?

Go back to the information you organized in Step 2. Does your answer make sense when you add it to the diagram or chart you made? Is it reasonable when you compare it to what you already know?

▌TRY IT OUT▐ ➡ **A student incorrectly solved the problem below. Find the mistake.**

1

3.N.25

Alfonzo has 38 yellow balloons, 22 red balloons, and 18 blue balloons for his party on Saturday. What is the **best** estimate of the total number of Alfonzo's balloons?

(A) 40 balloons

B 60 balloons

C 70 balloons

D 80 balloons

Compare this answer to the amount of yellow balloons Alfonzo has. Why is this answer unreasonable?

_____

_____

_____

Can you solve the problem another way?

In Step 3, you put together a problem-solving strategy and carried out your plan. Solving the problem another way can help you confirm that your answer is correct. If you solve the problem another way and don't get the same answer, check each of your computations.

In the space below, solve the problem another way.

Independent Practice

Use the 4-Step Method for Problem Solving to solve the problems in this section.

1

3.N.2

Alice gets this ticket at the bakery.

What number does Alice's ticket say?

A seventeen

B seventy-one

C one hundred seven

D one hundred seventy

hint ▷ *Make a place-value chart to organize the information from the problem.*

2

3.N.16

Tyrik needed an even number to win at bingo. Which number could be the winning number?

A 29

B 33

C 70

D 81

hint ▷ *Use paper to cover up the tens column so you can focus on the ones.*

3 What time does the clock below show?

3.M.9

A 2:06

B 2:30

C 6:03

D 6:15

hint ▶ *Find the hour first to eliminate incorrect answer choices.*

4 The pictogram shows the number of plants grown by Ms. Crest's science classes.

3.S.7

NUMBER OF PLANTS GROWN

Grade	Number of Plants
2	🌿 🌿
3	🌿 🌿 🌿 🌿
4	🌿 🌿
5	🌿 🌿 🌿

KEY	
🌿	= 5 plants

How many **more** plants did Grade 3 grow than Grade 4?

A 1

B 2

C 5

D 10

hint ▶ *Make sure you pay attention to the key in a pictograph. It will give you information you need to solve the problem.*

5 Which number would make the number sentence correct?

$$\boxed{} < 625$$

A 595

B 625

C 652

D 700

hint ▷ *Write out the problem in words to make sure you understand what it is asking for.*

6 What number makes both number sentences true?

$$45 \times \boxed{} = 45 \qquad 8 \times \boxed{} = 8$$

A 0

B 1

C 2

D 8

hint ▷ *After you select your response, ask yourself whether your answer is reasonable.*

7 Brianna wrote the number pattern below in her math notebook.

11, 15, 19, 23, 27,…

What rule did Brianna use to make her pattern?

A Add 4.

B Subtract 4.

C Divide by 4.

D Multiply by 4.

hint ▷ *In a number pattern, you can look at the changes between numbers to find the rule.*

8 The drawing below shows the houses in Matthew's neighborhood.

3.N.21

Which expression can be used to find the total number of houses in Matthew's neighborhood?

A $3 + 5$

B $5 \times 5 \times 5$

C $3 + 3 + 3$

D 3×5

 *Check your answer by solving the problem a different way.*

9 Which figure is $\frac{1}{3}$ shaded?

3.N.13

A

B

C

D

 *Think about how many of the shaded sections would fit in the whole shape.*

KAP Wrap

Robert solved the problem below. He incorrectly answered (A).

1

3.N.18

Maria collected 367 pennies for the penny drive. Malcolm collected 424 pennies. How many pennies did the two of them collect together?

(A) 57

B 143

C 781

D 791

424 − 367 = 57 pennies

Describe the error Robert made. _____

_____

_____

_____

What is the correct answer? _____

3 Lesson 3
OPEN-ENDED PROBLEMS

Focus Question

What do you need to do to earn full credit for open-ended problems?

Thinking KAP

Read the sample student work and thinking below. Label where the student completed each step of the 4-Step Method for Problem Solving.

1 Maya's teacher wrote this expression on the board.

3.N.9

$$8 + (4 + 6)$$

Which expression below <u>is the same</u> as Maya's teacher's expression?

IT ASKS ME TO FIND THE ANSWER THAT IS THE SAME AS THE EXPRESSION IN THE PROBLEM.

I KNOW THAT I CAN FIND OUT WHAT EACH EXPRESSION EQUALS IN ORDER TO COMPARE THEM.

All Things Equal Table

Question	$8 + (4 + 6)$	
A.	$8 + (6 + 6)$	18
B.	$(8 + 4) + 6$	20
C.	$8 × (4 + 6)$	18
D.	$8 + 8 + 8 + 8$	80
		32

DID I ANSWER THE RIGHT QUESTION?

Instruction

Open-Ended Problems

On the second day of the test, all the problems will be open-ended. Open-ended problems do not have answer choices. They may also ask you to show your work and explain your answer.

Some open-ended problems are worth three points. The rubric below shows how test graders score the three-point problems on the test.

3-Point Response	You show that you really understand the problem. You show all your work, and the work is all correct. You clearly explain how you solved the problem.
2-Point Response	You show that you mostly understand the problem. You show all your work, and the work is almost all correct. You explain how you solved the problem, but your explanation might not be clear.
1-Point Response	You show that you understand some of the problem. You show some of your work, but the work has some big mistakes in it. You don't completely explain how you solved the problem.
0-Point Response	You show that you don't understand the problem. You don't show any work. If you do, it is filled with mistakes. You don't explain how you solved the problem.

Think of the rubric this way:

• You get one point for a correct answer.

• You get one point for showing correct work when asked.

• You get one point for explaining your work when asked.

Short-Response Problems

Shorter problems will be worth only two points. The rubric below shows how test graders score the two-point problems on the test.

2-Point Response	You show that you really understand the problem. You show all your work, and the work is all correct. You clearly explain how you solved the problem.
1-Point Response	You show that you understand some of the problem. You find the correct answer, but you have not shown any work.
0-Point Response	You show that you don't understand the problem. You don't show any work. If you do, it is filled with mistakes. You don't explain how you solved the problem.

▮TRY IT OUT▮➤ **Use the rubric above to score the sample student work below.**

1 Janelle wrote the following number pattern with two blanks.

3.A.2

50, 43, 36, 29, __22__, 15, 8, __1__

Write the two missing numbers on the blank lines above.

Explain how you know what numbers are missing in the pattern.

The numbers go on the blanks.

I would give this student a _____ out of 2, because _____

_____ .

Say It! Support It! Explain It!

Use the strategy below to make sure you earn the highest possible score for open-ended problems.

Say it! Support it! Explain it!
• **Say it!** Write your answer in the blank provided.
• **Support it!** Show your work when you are asked.
• **Explain it!** Answer all questions in a way that shows the grader what you know.

TRY IT OUT ➡ **Use Say it! Support it! Explain it! to solve the problem below.**

2
3.N.22
Zory, Steve, and Risa are playing a card game. Zory deals out 15 cards equally to each player. In her first move, Risa takes two more cards from the deck. How many cards does Risa have after her first move?

Support
your answer here.

Show your work.

Say
your answer here.

Answer _____ cards

On the lines below, explain how you arrived at your answer.

Explain
your answer here.

_____

_____

_____

Use Say it! Support it! Explain it! to show your work for the problem below.

3

3.S.7

The bar graph below shows how many used batteries students collected for a recycling project.

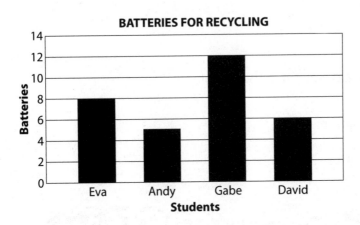

BATTERIES FOR RECYCLING

How many **more** batteries did Gabe collect than Eva?

Show your work.

Answer _____ batteries

On the lines below, explain how you got your answer.

_____

_____

_____

Use the questions below to look back at your answer.

☐ My answer is correct.

☐ My work helps the grader understand how I got the answer.

☐ My explanation is clear even to someone who doesn't know me.

Independent Practice

Use the 4-Step Method for Problem Solving and the strategies you have learned in this lesson to solve the problems in this section.

1 Use your ruler to help you solve this problem.

3.M.2

Noah found a caterpillar on a tree.

Using your ruler, find the length of the caterpillar in inches.

Answer _____ inches

On the lines below, explain how you found the length of the caterpillar.

_____

_____

_____

hint ▷ *The icon by the question number means that you should use your ruler for this problem.*

KAPLAN ADVANTAGE
NEW YORK MATHEMATICS GRADE 3

2 Jake drew this pattern using shapes.

3.A.2
3.G.3

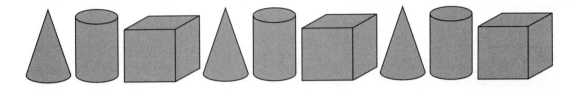

What is the name of the next shape in the pattern?

Answer _____

On the lines below, explain how you found the next shape in the pattern.

_____

_____

_____

_____

_____

hint ▷ *Think about what you need to know. Look at how the shapes are repeated in order to figure out the pattern.*

3 Clint drew this picture of clouds.

3.N.10

What fraction of the clouds shown are gray?

Answer _____

Shade the fraction bar to represent the fraction of **gray** clouds that have rain drops.

hint ▸ *Check to make sure that your answers are reasonable.*

4 Nora's basketball team scored 22 points in their game on Saturday, 26 points on Sunday, and 18 points on Monday. How many points did the team score in all?

3.N.18

Show your work.

Answer _____ points

hint ▸ *Check your answer by doing this problem in a different way.*

5

3.S.5

Diego sold T-shirts for his school's math club. The table below shows how many T-shirts he sold each week in February.

T-SHIRT SALES IN FEBRUARY

Week	T-Shirts Sold
Week 1	3
Week 2	6
Week 3	4
Week 4	3

How many T-shirts did Diego sell all together?

Show your work.

Answer _____ T-shirts

Complete the bar graph below to show the number of T-shirts sold each week.

Be sure to
- label the blank axis
- graph all the data

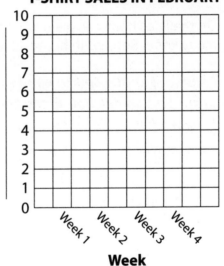

T-SHIRT SALES IN FEBRUARY

hint ▶ *Check off the data in the table as you make your graph, so you do not miss any information.*

KAP Wrap

Read the question and sample student answer below. Then, use the rubric on page 37 to score the student's work.

1

3.A.2

Samantha and Rob are making necklaces from knots. They each knot at the same pace. The chart below shows how many knots each necklace has as they work.

Samantha	Rob
5	9
10	14
20	24
25	?

Based on the pattern in the table, how many knots will Rob have when Samantha has 25?

Answer _____29_____ knots

On the lines below, explain what rule you used to find how many knots Rob has in his necklace.

I added 4 knots to the number that Samantha had in order to find out how many knots Rob had in his necklace. I checked the rule by trying it for each row.

I would give this student a _____ out of 2, because _____

_____

_____

_____

UNIT 2 Strategies for Algebra and Number Sense

I USE PATTERNS TO MAKE ART.

ARTIST

1 Lesson 1
PATTERNS

Focus Question

How can you find the missing shape or number in a pattern?

Thinking KAP

Kim's teacher is passing out hats that tell students what parts they will play in an upcoming skit. Kim notices a pattern.

Describe the pattern Kim notices.

_____

_____

Kim is about to get the next hat. If the pattern continues, what kind of hat will she get?

_____

Shape Patterns

Every pattern follows a rule. To find a rule that describes a shape pattern, look for one of the following:

- **repeating:** a series of figures that repeat the same order

- **growing:** each figure is larger than the one before it, or contains more shapes

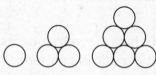

- **shrinking:** each figure is smaller than the one before it, or contains fewer shapes

▌TRY IT OUT▐ ➡ Look for repeating, growing, or shrinking objects, then draw the missing figures in each pattern.

1. ◯ ▢ ◇ ◯ ◯ ▢ ◇ ◯ __ __

2. ▢ △ ◯ ▢ △ __ ▢ __ ◯

3.    _____

Number Patterns

Patterns can also be made of numbers, instead of shapes. To find a rule that describes a number pattern, look at whether the numbers increase or decrease, and by how much from one to the next.

Unlock the Pattern

- If the numbers increase, the pattern uses +.
- If the numbers decrease, the pattern uses −.

Unlock the Pattern by finding the rule for each of the patterns below. Use the rule to extend each pattern.

Pattern	Increase (+) or Decrease (−)?	By how much?
1, 3, 5, 7, 9, _____		
30, 25, 20, 15, 10, _____		

Eliminating

Sometimes, you will be asked to identify a pattern's rule from a list of choices. Test each rule to see if it describes the whole pattern.

ITRY IT OUTI ➤ **Test each rule for the pattern in this problem.**

1 Edwin writes the number pattern below.

3.A.2

$$23, 19, 15, 11, 7, \_\_\_\_\_$$

Which rule can be used to find the next number in the pattern?

A Add 7.

B Subtract 7.

C Add 4.

D Subtract 4.

Test each rule. If a rule does not work for the entire pattern, eliminate it.

- Does the rule in (A) work? _____
- Does the rule in (B) work? _____
- Does the rule in (C) work? _____
- Does the rule in (D) work? _____

Patterns in a Table

Patterns can appear in tables, too. To find a rule that describes a pattern in a table, look for a relationship in each row. The relationship should be the same for each row of the table.

Cindy's Age	Tom's Age
2 —+10→ 12	
5 —+10→ 15	
7 —+10→ 17	
8 —+10→ 18	

▌TRY IT OUT▌➡ **Use the patterns and relationships in the table to solve the problem.**

2
3.A.2 Maria makes and delivers sandwiches for office workers. The table below shows the prices Maria charges for different-sized orders.

Number of Sandwiches Ordered	Price for Sandwiches and Delivery
3	$7.00
6	$10.00
9	?
12	$16.00

Based on the pattern in the table, what does Maria charge to make and deliver 9 sandwiches?

A $9.00

B $12.00

C $13.00

D $17.00

- Look for a relationship in each row.
- Draw the relationship using an arrow.
- Make sure the relationship is the same for each row.

Explaining the Rule

When asked to describe a rule in a pattern or to explain how you know how to complete a pattern, use mathematical words and be specific.

Pattern	Explain the Rule		
	Use a Math Action Word	Tell What	Tell Where
54, 45, 36, 27, 18, 9, 0	subtract	9	from the previous number
△ ○ △ ○	repeat	the shapes "triangle and circle"	one after another
○ ○○○ ○○○○	add	a row with 1 more circle than the last row	to the bottom of each new figure

┃TRY IT OUT┃➤ **Describe the rules for the patterns below. Use math action words, and tell what and where.**

Pattern	Explain the Rule
25, 50, 75, 100, 125, 150	
☐ ○ ☐ ○	
1,000, 900, 800, 700, 600	

Independent Practice

Use the 4-Step Method for Problem Solving and the strategies you have learned in this lesson to solve the problems in this section.

1 What are the next two numbers in the pattern below?

3.A.2

18, 22, 26, 30, _____, _____

A   28, 32
B   32, 36
C   34, 36
D   34, 38

hint *Determine whether the numbers are increasing or decreasing.*

2 Which rule can be used to find the next number in the pattern below?

3.A.2

49, 42, 35, 28, 21, _____

A   Add 7.
B   Subtract 7.
C   Add 14.
D   Subtract 14.

hint *Try each rule and eliminate those that do not work.*

3 How many circles will be in the **fourth** figure in the pattern below?

3.A.2

A   3
B   4
C   5
D   6

hint *Look for growing or shrinking in the pattern.*

KAPLAN ADVANTAGE
NEW YORK MATHEMATICS GRADE 3

4

3.A.2

Shawn and Lianne have the same birthday. The ages of Shawn and Lianne as they grow older are shown in the table below.

AGES (IN YEARS)

Shawn	Lianne
7	4
11	8
16	13
18	?

Based on the pattern in the table, how old will Lianne be when Shawn is 18?

Answer _____ years old

On the lines below, describe the rule you can use to find Lianne's age if you know Shawn's age.

_____

_____

_____

_____

hint *Look for a relationship in the rows.*

5 The number pattern below has two missing numbers.

3.A.2

700, 650, 600, 550, _____ , 450, 400, _____

Write the two missing numbers on the blank lines in the pattern above.

On the lines below, explain how you know what numbers are missing in the pattern.

_____

_____

_____

_____

_____

On the lines below, write a different set of numbers that uses the same rule as the pattern above. Do not use any of the numbers from the pattern above.

Pattern _____ , _____ , _____ , _____

hint ⟩ *In your explanation, use a math action word, and tell what and where.*

KAPLAN ADVANTAGE
NEW YORK MATHEMATICS GRADE 3

© 2010 Kaplan, Inc.

6

3.A.2

Eleanor drew the repeating pattern of shapes shown below.

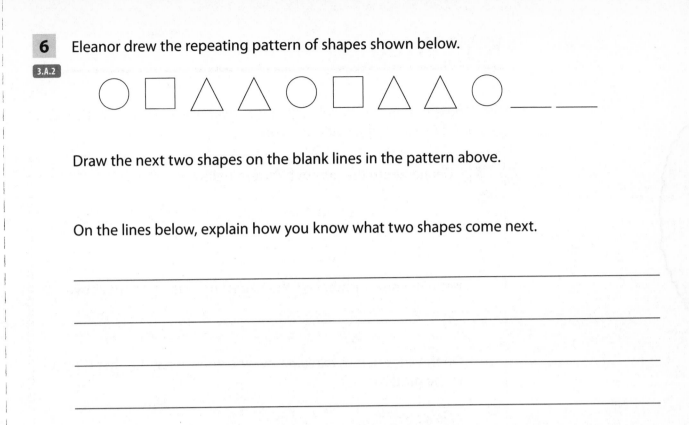

Draw the next two shapes on the blank lines in the pattern above.

On the lines below, explain how you know what two shapes come next.

_____

_____

_____

_____

In the space below, draw the **17th** shape in the pattern.

hint *Keep drawing the pattern until you reach a total of 17 shapes.*

UNIT 2 ● ② ③

KAP Wrap

Read the question and sample student answer below. Then, use the rubric on page 37 to score the student's work.

---

1 Gerald wrote the number pattern below.

3.A.2

21, 18, 15, 12, ___*9*___

Write the next number on the blank line in the pattern above.

On the lines below, explain how you know what number is next in the pattern.

Go down.

_____

_____

I would give this student a _____ out of 2, because _____

_____

_____

_____

2 Lesson 2
PLACE VALUE AND WHOLE NUMBERS

Focus Question

How does place value determine the value of a digit in a number?

Thinking KAP

At a café, you see the meal options shown below. Circle the meal that costs **more** than $8 but **less** than $13.

Imagine that you want to pay for your meal with the fewest number of bills possible. You have ten-dollar bills and one-dollar bills. In the space below, draw the bills you could use to pay for the meal you circled.

Instruction

The Value of a Digit

Which would you rather have: one $1-bill or one $10-bill? Both bills are a single piece of paper, but one has a much greater value.

Likewise, think about the number 445. The first 4 in the number stands for 4 *hundreds*, or 400. The second 4 stands for 4 *tens*, or 40.

Place-Value Charts

A place-value chart shows you the value of each digit in a number. Use the place-value chart below to answer the following questions.

100s	10s	1s
8	3	6

- Which digit is in the tens place in the number 836? _____
- What is the value of the digit 8 in this number? _____

ⅠTRY IT OUTⅠ➡   **Compare 392 to 376.**

Write each number in the place-value chart below. Then, compare the numbers from left to right.

100s	10s	1s

- Compare hundreds: which digit is greater? _____
- Compare tens: which digit is greater? _____
- Which number is greater? _____

Writing Numbers in Expanded and Word Forms

Most numbers appear in **standard form**. However, you can change numbers to **expanded form** by writing out the value of each digit.

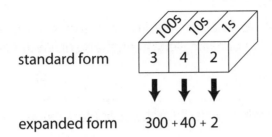

standard form

expanded form $300 + 40 + 2$

You can also write numbers in **word form**.

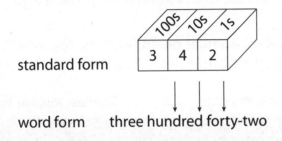

standard form

word form   three hundred forty-two

ITRY IT OUTI ➡ **Complete the table below.**

Standard Form	Expanded Form	Word Form
283		two hundred eighty-three
	$600 + 5$	six hundred five
719		

Creating Numbers

On the Math Test, you may be required to make new 3-digit numbers out of individual digits. For example, you might be given the digits below.

1,   5,   9

To make new 3-digit numbers, think about place value:

- To make the **largest number possible,** start by putting the largest digit in the place with the greatest value—the hundreds place. The next largest value goes in the tens place, and the smallest digit goes in the ones place.

- To make the **smallest number possible**, do the opposite. The smallest digit will go in the hundreds place, and the largest digit in the ones place.

Largest Number Possible   **Smallest Number Possible**

100s	10s	1s		100s	10s	1s
9	5	1		1	5	9

▌TRY IT OUT▐ ➡ **Solve the problem below.**

1

3.N.3

Ella draws the numbers below from a deck of cards.

4,   7,   8

She uses the numbers on the cards to make larger numbers. What is the **largest** 3-digit number Ella can make with 7 in the ones place?

A 487

B 748

C 847

D 874

Completing Number Sentences

The symbols below show relationships between numbers in sentences.

$<$ (less than) $>$ (greater than) $=$ (equal to)

Write a symbol in each box below to make the number sentences true.

4 ☐ 7   3 ☐ 3   8 ☐ 2

Eliminating

Eliminating is a helpful strategy when you must choose a number to correctly complete a number sentence. To use Eliminating with number sentence problems, do the following:

- Determine whether you are looking for a number that is greater than or less than the number in the number sentence.

- Look at the hundreds place for each answer choice. Eliminate choices in which the hundreds place is not greater than or less than the hundreds place of the number in the number sentence.

- Continue by looking at the tens place to eliminate additional answer choices, then by looking at the ones place, until you have eliminated all but the correct answer.

▌TRY IT OUT▐➡   **Eliminate to solve the problem below.**

2   Sam wrote the number sentence below.

3.A.1

☐ $>$ 396

Which number belongs in the box to make the number sentence true?

A 382

B 394

C 396

D 398

- Compare hundreds: what can you eliminate? Why? _____

_____

- Compare tens: what can you eliminate? Why? _____

_____

- Compare ones: what can you eliminate? Why? _____

_____

Independent Practice

Use the 4-Step Method for Problem Solving and the strategies you have learned in this lesson to solve the problems in this section.

1 What is the value of the 2 in the number 425?

3.N.4

 A 2

 B 20

 C 25

 D 200

hint ▸ *Draw a place-value chart and write the number in expanded form.*

2 Which of these number sentences is correct?

3.A.1

 A $3 < 7$

 B $6 < 3$

 C $7 > 7$

 D $8 > 9$

hint ▸ *Read each number sentence and eliminate those that are not correct.*

3 Cecil took 239 steps from the classroom to the cafeteria. Renee took 312 steps, and Kelsi took 256. Which statement about the number of steps taken is correct?

3.A.1

 A $239 > 256$

 B $256 > 239$

 C $312 < 239$

 D $312 < 256$

hint ▸ *Use place-value charts to compare the numbers in each answer choice. Eliminate number sentences that are incorrect.*

4 James put his dog Tippen on the scale below.

3.N.2

How many pounds does Tippen weigh?

A twenty-three

B two hundred three

C two hundred thirty

D twenty-three hundred

hint ▶ *Write each of the answer choices in standard form to find the one that matches the number on the scale.*

5 Ravi writes the number sentence below.

3.A.1

$$265 > \underline{\quad\quad}$$

Which number can go on the line to make the number sentence true?

A 237

B 273

C 312

D 344

hint ▶ *Eliminate answer choices that do not make the number sentence true.*

6 Mr. Sung ordered red and blue balloons for a school party, as shown on the form below.

3.N.3

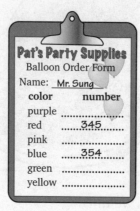

Pat's Party Supplies
Balloon Order Form
Name: _Mr. Sung_

color	number
purple	....
red	.....345.....
pink	....
blue	.....354.....
green	....
yellow	....

Which color balloon did Mr. Sung order the **most** of?

Answer _____

On the lines below, explain how you know which number is **greater**.

_____

_____

_____

_____

hint ▶ *Use a place-value chart to help you compare the number of balloons of each color.*

KAPLAN ADVANTAGE
NEW YORK MATHEMATICS GRADE 3

© 2010 Kaplan, Inc.

7 Jenna plays a number game. She uses the numbers below to make larger numbers.

3.N.3

2,   6,   8

What is the **smallest** number Jenna can make?

Answer _____

What is the **largest** number Jenna can make?

Answer _____

What is the **largest** number Jenna can make with the 8 in the tens place?

Answer _____

hint *For the third question, draw a place-value chart and place 8 in the tens place.*

KAP Wrap

Read the question and sample student answer below. Then, use the rubric on page 36 to score the student's work.

1

3.N.3

The distance from LaGuardia Airport to Rochester is three hundred forty-five miles. The distance from LaGuardia Airport to Buffalo is four hundred seven miles.

The traffic sign below will be posted at LaGuardia Airport. Complete the sign by writing the driving distances to Rochester and Buffalo in standard form on the blank lines.

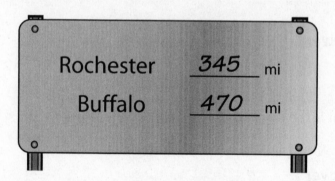

Rochester _345_ mi

Buffalo _470_ mi

Which city is farther from LaGuardia Airport?

Show your work.

	100s	10s	1s
Rochester	3	4	5
Buffalo	4	7	0

Answer _____Buffalo_____

I would give this student a _____ out of 3, because _____

_____

_____

_____

KAPLAN ADVANTAGE
NEW YORK MATHEMATICS GRADE 3

© 2010 Kaplan, Inc.

3 Lesson 3
FRACTIONS

Focus Question
How do you tell what fraction represents part of a whole or a group?

Thinking KAP

All of the animals on Farmer Jane's farm are shown below.

Complete the statements below to make them match the picture above.

• There is _____ pig out of _____ total animals on the farm.

• There is _____ spotted cow out of _____ total cows on the farm.

Instruction

Fractions as Parts of a Whole

Fractions describe the relationship between parts and totals.

$$\frac{\text{numerator}}{\text{denominator}} = \frac{\text{number of parts you're talking about}}{\text{total number of equal parts the whole is divided into}}$$

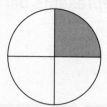 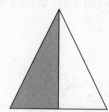

1 part is shaded
out of 4 equal parts

$\frac{1}{4}$ of the whole
circle is shaded

1 part is shaded
out of 2 equal parts

$\frac{1}{2}$ of the whole
triangle is shaded

▌TRY IT OUT▐ ➡ **Draw a line to match each figure with the fraction that describes it.**

1. 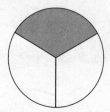 $\frac{1}{5}$

2. 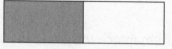 $\frac{1}{3}$

3.  $\frac{1}{2}$

Representing Unit Fractions

A **unit fraction** shows the size of one equal part of a whole. The **numerator** of a unit fraction is always one, because there is only one shaded part. The **denominator** describes the number of equal parts the total is divided into.

You can draw unit fractions as parts of a circle.

$\dfrac{1}{3}$ $\qquad\qquad\qquad$ $\dfrac{1}{6}$ $\qquad\qquad\qquad$ $\dfrac{1}{10}$

❚TRY IT OUT❚➡ **Write the unit fraction under each circle diagram.**

    ⬤

_____   _____   _____

You can also show unit fractions as parts of a bar.

$\dfrac{1}{2}$ $\qquad\qquad\qquad$ $\dfrac{1}{3}$ $\qquad\qquad\qquad$ $\dfrac{1}{10}$

❚TRY IT OUT❚➡ **Divide and shade a fraction bar to represent each unit fraction.**

1. $\dfrac{1}{4}$

2. $\dfrac{1}{5}$

3. $\dfrac{1}{6}$

Equal Parts

You know that a fraction represents part of a whole. You also know that the denominator represents the total number of equal parts in the whole.

Each of the rectangles below has six total parts. Each of them also has one part shaded. However, only one of them is $\frac{1}{6}$ shaded.

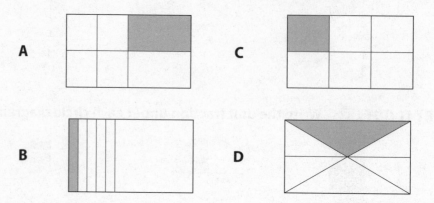

Only rectangle C is $\frac{1}{6}$ shaded, as it is the only rectangle divided into six **equal** parts.

❙ TRY IT OUT ❙▶ Tell whether each figure below is divided into equal parts. If the parts are equal, write the fraction that represents the shaded part.

1.

☐ parts not equal

☐ parts equal, fraction: _____

2.

☐ parts not equal

☐ parts equal, fraction: _____

3.

☐ parts not equal

☐ parts equal, fraction: _____

KAPLAN ADVANTAGE
NEW YORK MATHEMATICS GRADE 3

© 2010 Kaplan, Inc.

Fractions as Parts of a Group

Fractions are not always part of a circle or a bar or any other whole unit. Sometimes, a fraction is part of a group or set:

$$\frac{\text{numerator}}{\text{denominator}} = \frac{\text{number you're talking about}}{\text{total number in the group}}$$

In the Thinking KAP activity, you saw a group of farm animals.

1 out of the 5 animals was a pig.

1 out of the 4 cows was spotted.

$$\frac{\text{number of pigs}}{\text{total number of animals}} = \frac{1}{5}$$

$$\frac{\text{number of spotted cows}}{\text{total number of cows}} = \frac{1}{4}$$

▌TRY IT OUT▐ ➡ **Solve the problems below.**

1 Brianna has the 4 socks shown below.

`3.N.10`

What fraction of Brianna's socks are black?

A $\frac{1}{4}$

B $\frac{1}{3}$

C $\frac{2}{4}$

D $\frac{4}{1}$

2 Draw a ring around $\frac{1}{6}$ of the set of shoes shown below.

`3.N.11`

Independent Practice

Use the 4-Step Method for Problem Solving and the strategies you have learned in this lesson to solve the problems in this section.

1 Which figure is $\frac{1}{4}$ shaded?

`3.N.13`

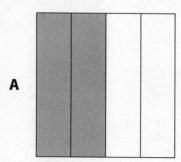 A

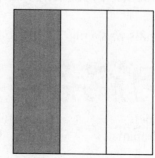 C

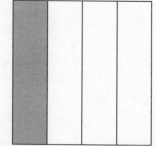 B

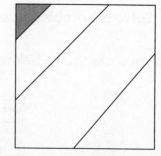 D

hint *Eliminate figures that do not show one out of four equal parts shaded.*

2 Mackenzie wrote the number sentence below.

`3.A.1`

$$\square > \frac{1}{4}$$

Which fraction goes in the box to make the number sentence true?

A $\frac{1}{3}$

B $\frac{1}{4}$

C $\frac{1}{5}$

D $\frac{1}{6}$

hint *What does the symbol > mean?*

3 The Harris family owns the 5 backpacks shown below.

3.N.10

What fraction of the Harris family's backpacks are gray?

A $\frac{1}{5}$

B $\frac{1}{4}$

C $\frac{2}{5}$

D $\frac{5}{1}$

hint *The fraction should tell how many backpacks out of the 5 are gray.*

4 Billy has placed olives on 1 out of the 3 pizzas shown below.

3.N.10

On what fraction of the set of 3 pizzas did Billy place olives?

A $\frac{1}{5}$

B $\frac{1}{4}$

C $\frac{1}{3}$

D $\frac{1}{2}$

hint *The denominator tells the total number of items in a group.*

UNIT 2 ① ②

5 There are three T-shirts and three pairs of pants shown below.

3.N.10

What fraction of the set of clothes above are gray?

Answer _____

What fraction of the set of **shirts** above are black?

Answer _____

Draw a ring around $\frac{1}{2}$ of the set of gloves shown below.

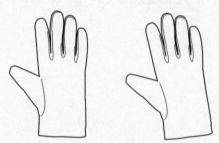

hint ▸ *Count the total number of items in each set to get your denominators.*

6 There are 2 rectangles shown below.

3.N.13

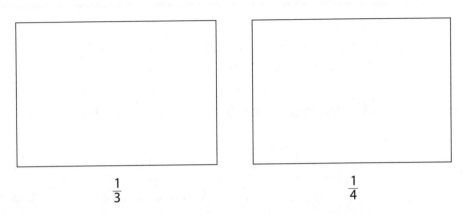

$$\frac{1}{3}$$ $$\frac{1}{4}$$

Divide and shade each rectangle to match the fraction written underneath.

Explain why the diagram below does **not** show $\frac{1}{4}$.

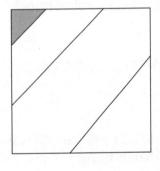

_____

_____

_____

_____

hint *The more pieces you divide a figure into, the smaller the pieces will be.*

KAP Wrap

Read the question and sample student answer below. Then, use the rubric on page 37 to score the student's work.

1 Mr. Johnson cut three pies as shown in the figures below.

3.N.11

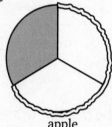
apple

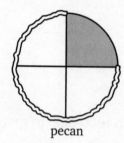
pecan

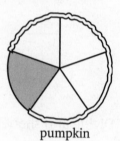
pumpkin

Mr. Johnson wants to give his son $\frac{1}{4}$ of a whole pie. Which pie should he take a slice from?

Answer _____pecan_____

Orlando had a piece that was $\frac{1}{3}$ of a whole pie. What kind of pie did Orlando have?

Answer _____pumpkin_____

I would give this student a _____ out of 2, because _____

_____

_____

_____

MPT Mini Practice Test 1

Mini Practice Test 1

1. Ⓐ Ⓑ Ⓒ Ⓓ   5. Ⓐ Ⓑ Ⓒ Ⓓ   9. Ⓐ Ⓑ Ⓒ Ⓓ

2. Ⓐ Ⓑ Ⓒ Ⓓ   6. Ⓐ Ⓑ Ⓒ Ⓓ   10. Ⓐ Ⓑ Ⓒ Ⓓ

3. Ⓐ Ⓑ Ⓒ Ⓓ   7. Ⓐ Ⓑ Ⓒ Ⓓ   11. Ⓐ Ⓑ Ⓒ Ⓓ

4. Ⓐ Ⓑ Ⓒ Ⓓ   8. Ⓐ Ⓑ Ⓒ Ⓓ   12. Ⓐ Ⓑ Ⓒ Ⓓ

Your answers for questions 13–14 should be written in the test booklet.

1 Drew writes the number sentence below.

$$476 > \boxed{}$$

Which number belongs in the box to make the number sentence true?

A 475

B 476

C 477

D 478

2 Reginald has a group of marbles, shown below.

What fraction of Reginald's marbles are striped?

A $\frac{1}{4}$

B $\frac{2}{4}$

C $\frac{3}{4}$

D $\frac{4}{1}$

Go On

3 Phillip had two hundred and four stickers in a binder. What is another way to write two hundred and four?

A 204

B 220

C 240

D 244

4 Makia writes the number pattern below.

$$17, 23, 29, 35, 41, \underline{\hspace{2cm}}$$

Which rule can be used to find the next number in the pattern?

A Multiply by 3.

B Add 6.

C Subtract 6.

D Divide by 3.

5 Eric writes the number sentence below.

$$\square > \frac{1}{4}$$

Which number belongs in the box to make the number sentence true?

A $\frac{1}{3}$

B $\frac{1}{4}$

C $\frac{1}{5}$

D $\frac{1}{6}$

6 Which figure is $\frac{1}{5}$ shaded?

A

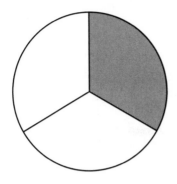

C

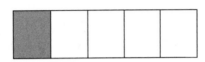

B

D

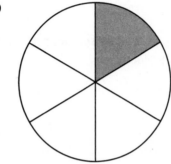

7 Justin writes the number pattern below.

47, 39, 31, 23, 15, _____

Which rule can be used to find the next number in the pattern?

A Add 8.

B Add 17.

C Divide by 8.

D Subtract 8.

Go On

8 Erin is arranging the number flashcards shown below.

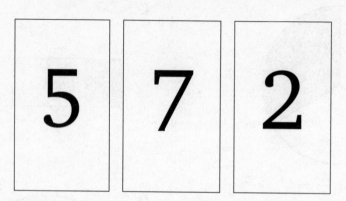

Using only these three flashcards, what is the **greatest** number Erin can make that has a 5 in the ones place?

A 752

B 725

C 527

D 275

9 Helene starting baking muffins at 4:00 P.M. She took them out of the oven after $\frac{1}{4}$ hour. At what time did Helene take the muffins out of the oven?

A 4:04 P.M.

B 4:10 P.M.

C 4:15 P.M.

D 4:30 P.M.

10 Which figure is $\frac{1}{4}$ shaded?

A

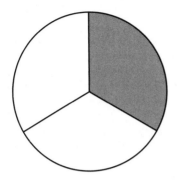

C

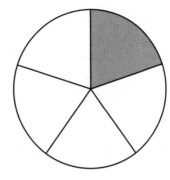

B

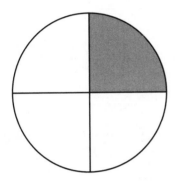

D

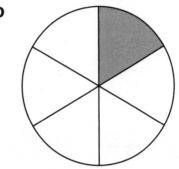

11 A movie theater had 592 seats. What is another way to write 592?

    A five hundred ninety-two

    B five hundred twenty-nine

    C fifty ninety-two

    D fifty-nine two

12 What is the value of the 4 in 647?

    A 4

    B 40

    C 400

    D 4,000

Go On

13 Giles used blocks to make the pattern below.

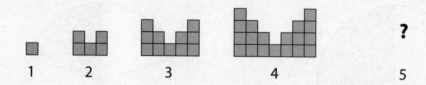

1   2   3   4   5

In the space below, draw the 5th figure in the pattern.

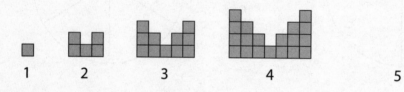

1   2   3   4   5

On the lines below, describe the rule you used to find the 5th figure in Giles's pattern.

_____

_____

_____

_____

KAPLAN ADVANTAGE
NEW YORK MATHEMATICS GRADE 3

© 2010 Kaplan, Inc.

14   There are three fish shown below.

What fraction of the fish above are not gray?

Answer _____

What fraction of the gray fish above have stripes?

Answer _____

Draw a ring around $\frac{1}{4}$ of the crabs shown below.

STOP

Reflection

Reflect on your work on the Mini Practice Test by completing the table below. First, rate each question by circling either "Comfortable" or "Challenging." Then, under the "How did you figure out the answer?" column, write the name of the strategy you used to answer each question.

Question	Rate this question!	How did you figure out the answer?
1	Comfortable Challenging	
2	Comfortable Challenging	
3	Comfortable Challenging	
4	Comfortable Challenging	
5	Comfortable Challenging	
6	Comfortable Challenging	
7	Comfortable Challenging	
8	Comfortable Challenging	
9	Comfortable Challenging	
10	Comfortable Challenging	
11	Comfortable Challenging	
12	Comfortable Challenging	

Reflect on Open-Ended Problems

For each problem you got right, describe what really helped you to solve the problem.

- Did you read carefully?

- Did you check your work?

- Did you think back to mistakes you had made before and avoid them?

For each problem you got wrong, describe the error that you made. Based on your answers, give yourself some advice for Test Day.

Question	What did you do to solve the problem that really helped you? or What error did you make?	What advice do you have for yourself on Test Day?
13		
14		

UNIT 3 Strategies for Operations

HOT DOG VENDOR

1 Lesson 1
PARTS AND TOTALS

Focus Question
How does a part-total bar help you choose an operation?

Thinking KAP

Sam walked 8 city blocks to the library. He walked another 5 blocks to the basketball court.

What operation can you use to find the total number of blocks Sam walked?

_____

Write and solve the number sentence on the line below.

_____

How did you decide which operation to use? _____

_____

Instruction

Part-Total Bars

Many of the problems on the Math Test ask you to work with parts and totals. Drawing a part-total bar can help you analyze the important information in these problems. This kind of diagram helps you see how the parts and totals are related.

Part-Total Bars
• Draw a bar to represent the total. Label the total, if known.
• Separate the bar to represent the parts. Label the parts that are known.
• Use the given information to identify the missing parts or totals.

TRY IT OUT ➡ **Use a part-total bar to analyze the important information in the problem below.**

First, underline the words in the problem that tell you about the total.

1   Mr. Forrest has a total of 68 books in his classroom library. He gives
3.N.18   31 books to Ms. Jenkins for her library. How many books does
         Mr. Forrest have left?

A 27   **C** 79

B 37   **D** 99

w label the total in the blank below.

_____ *books*

Divide the bar above to show the parts. Label any parts that you know.

Choosing an Operation

To use your part-total bar to choose an operation, ask yourself:

- What do you know?
- What do you need?
- How can you use what you know to find what you need?

When You Know the <u>Parts</u> and You Need to Find the <u>Total</u>

When the parts are different sizes, you can add to find the total.

$3	$4	$_____

When the parts are the same size, you can multiply the value of one of the parts by the total number of parts.

$2	$2	$2	$_____

▌TRY IT OUT▐➧ **Use a part-total bar to analyze the important information.**

2

3.N.18

Barbara collected 341 United States stamps and 476 international stamps. How many total stamps are there in Barbara's collection?

A 701   **C** 778

B 717   **D** 817

Draw a part-total bar to analyze the important information.

What do you know? _____

What do you need? _____

How can you use what you know to find what you need? _____

When You Know the Total and You Need to Find the Parts

You can subtract the part you know from the total to find a missing part.

$10	$_____	$15

When you know how many parts the total is divided into, and you know the parts are equal, you can divide the total by the number of parts to find the size of each part.

$_____	$_____	$_____	$9

▌TRY IT OUT▐ ▶ **Use a part-total bar to solve the problem below.**

3
3.N.22
Tamika had 8 dog treats. She gave the same number of treats to each of her 4 dogs. How many treats did each dog get?

A 2   **C** 12

B 4   **D** 32

Draw a part-total bar to analyze the important information.

What do you know? _____

What do you need? _____

How can you use what you know to find what you need? _____

_____

Comparing: What's the Difference?

Some problems will give you a set of numbers and will ask you to compare them. These problems often include clue words like *how many more* or *how much less*.

This type of problem is NOT about parts and totals. Instead, you have two totals and you need to compare them. You can draw two total bars to find the difference.

For example, if you are 8 years old and your sister is 14 years old, how much older is your sister than you?

```
┌─────────────────────────────────────┐
│            14 years                  │
└─────────────────────────────────────┘
                    └──────┬──────┘
                        ? years

┌──────────────────────┐
│       8 years        │         6 years
└──────────────────────┘
```

Subtract to find this **difference.**

TRY IT OUT ➤ **Use total bars to solve the problem below.**

4

3.N.18

Oliver's soccer team earned $83 from a bake sale on Saturday. On Sunday, the team earned $141. How much **more** did the team earn on Sunday than on Saturday?

What words in the problem tell you what information you are looking for?

_____

_____

Draw two total bars to analyze the important information.

What operation can you use to solve this problem? _____

Write a number sentence for this problem: _____

Independent Practice

Use the 4-Step Method for Problem Solving and the strategies you have learned in this lesson to solve the problems in this section.

1

3.N.19

The school band sold 9 sets of tickets. Each set contained 8 tickets. How many tickets did the band sell in all?

A 1

B 17

C 64

D 72

hint ▶ *Create a part-total bar. What do you know? What do you need to find out?*

2

3.N.18

Ms. Harling drove 235 miles to visit her cousin. Mr. Pasternak drove 681 miles to visit his grandmother. How many **more** miles did Mr. Pasternak drive than Ms. Harling?

A 394

B 414

C 446

D 456

hint ▶ *This problem is asking you to compare two numbers.*

3

3.N.24

Sam has made 40 paper cranes. She wants to give the same number of cranes to each of 8 friends. Which expression can Sam use to find out how many cranes each friend gets?

A $40 + 8$

B $40 - 8$

C 40×8

D $40 \div 8$

hint ▶ *Make a bar. Then, separate it into the given number of parts.*

4 There are 49 books about soccer, 111 books about baseball, and 67 books about football in the sports section of the Alamedas Elementary School library. How many total books are there in the sports section of the library?

3.N.18

   A 117

   B 227

   C 238

   D 307

hint *What do you know? What do you need?*

5 Judah plants 6 rows of vegetables. He puts 9 plants in each row. Which expression can be used to find the number of plants Judah has planted?

3.N.24

   A 6×9

   B $9 - 6$

   C $6 + 6$

   D $6 \div 9$

hint *Use a part-total bar to help you identify the best operation.*

6 Mr. Slate has a box of 70 markers. He wants to put an equal number of mark   in 7 boxes. How many markers will be in each box?

3.N.22

   A 7

   B 10

   C 63

   D 77

hint *Use a part-total bar to help you select the best operation.*

UNIT 3

7 A principal ordered party hats for the fifth-grade graduation party, as shown on the order form below.

3.N.18

PARTY HATS

Blue: __281__ hats
Yellow: __346__ hats

How many hats did the principal order in all?

A 65

B 527

C 605

D 627

hint ▷ *Use the information in the picture to help you complete a part-total bar.*

8 Elmira is making gift bags for 12 of her friends. If she wants to put 5 toys in each bag, how many toys does she need to buy?

3.N.20

A 48

B 50

C 56

D 60

hint ▷ *How many parts does the problem describe? How big is each part?*

9 Kevin scored 399 points during this year's basketball season. Leandra scored 572 points during the season. How many **more** points did Leandra score than Kevin?

3.N.18

Show your work.

Answer _____ points

hint ▷ *The words in the question will help you de   which operation you need to perform.*

10 Reina had 36 strawberries. She put an   ual number of strawberries into 6 different fruit cups. How many strawberries did Rei   ut into each fruit cup?

3.N.22

Show your work.

Answer _____ strawberries

hint ▷ *The problem tells you the total and the number of equal parts.*

KAP Wrap

Read the question and sample student answer below. Then, use the rubric on page 37 to score the student's work.

1

3.N.22

Miranda has 28 note cards. She gives an equal number of note cards to 4 of her friends. How many note cards does each friend get if Miranda gives away all her note cards?

Show your work.

28 note cards	4 note cards	? note cards

$$\begin{array}{r} \overset{1}{28} \\ +4 \\ \hline 32 \end{array}$$

Answer _____32_____ note cards

I would give this student a _____ out of 2, because _____

_____

_____

_____

2 Lesson 2
NUMBER PROPERTIES

Focus Question
What rules make solving math problems easier?

Thinking KAP

The penguin house at the zoo houses emperor penguins and king penguins. When she visited, Satya saw 12 emperor penguins. She didn't see any king penguins.

What expression can Satya use to show the total number of penguins she saw?

_____

How many penguins did Satya see? _____

Instruction

Some Properties of Zero and One

The numbers 0 and 1 work in special ways when they're used in multiplication expressions. Knowing the properties of these numbers can help you solve problems quickly and accurately on a test.

Identity Property of Multiplication

Whenever you multiply a number by the number 1, you always get the same number you started with.

For example, $2 \times 1 = 2$, and $20,000 \times 1 = 20,000$.

Zero Property of Multiplication

Whenever you multiply a number by 0, your answer will always be 0.
For example, $2 \times 0 = 0$, and $20,000 \times 0 = 0$.

▌TRY IT OUT▌➧ Use what you know about these properties of 0 and 1 to make each number sentence true.

1. $14 \times \underline{\hspace{1cm}} = 0$

2. $\underline{\hspace{1cm}} \times 96 = 96$

3. $1 \times 0 = \underline{\hspace{1cm}}$

4. $\underline{\hspace{1cm}} \times 0 = 0$

5. $25 \times 0 = \underline{\hspace{1cm}}$

6. $15 \times 1 = \underline{\hspace{1cm}}$

7. $3,500 \times 1 = \underline{\hspace{1cm}}$

8. $18 \times \underline{\hspace{1cm}} = 18$

9. $1 \times \underline{\hspace{1cm}} = 1$

10. $0 \times 8 = \underline{\hspace{1cm}}$

11. $\underline{\hspace{1cm}} \times 9 = 0$

12. $1 \times \underline{\hspace{1cm}} = 12$

The Commutative Property

When you solve a multiplication or addition problem, the order of the numbers in the problem isn't important. You can rearrange the numbers, and the expression will still have the same value. Look at the examples below:

$$4 + 5 + 6 = 6 + 5 + 4 = 5 + 6 + 4$$

$$2 \times 8 = 8 \times 2$$

You can use the commutative property to move numbers around within a problem. Just remember that this property only applies to multiplication and addition—the numbers in division and subtraction problems need to stay where they are.

⏵TRY IT OUT⏵ **Use what you know about the commutative property to make each number sentence true.**

1. $6 + 1 = 1 +$ _____

2. $9 \times$ _____ $\times 4 = 4 \times 9 \times 3$

3. $15 + 10 + 36 = 10 + 36 +$ _____

4. $0 + 4 =$ _____ $+ 0$

5. $12 + 1 =$ _____ $+ 1$

6. $10 \times 4 \times 2 = 4 \times 10 \times$ _____

7. $2 +$ _____ $+ 3 = 3 + 4 +$ _____

8. _____ $\times 7 = 7 \times 5$

9. $41 +$ _____ $= 17 + 41$

10. $5 \times 4 \times 5 = 4 \times$ _____ $\times 5$

11. $3 + 65 + 7 = 7 + 3 +$ _____

12. $1 \times 16 = 16 \times$ _____

13. _____ $+ 9 + 6 = 9 + 7 + 6$

14. _____ $\times 3 \times 7 = 9 \times 7 \times$ _____

Backsolving

Some questions on a test will ask you to select the answer choice that helps you to make a number sentence correct. Often, you'll be able to use what you know about number properties and math facts to answer these questions. However, if you are not sure how to answer the question, Backsolving can help you.

Backsolving
Put each answer choice back into the problem. If an answer choice does not make the problem true, you can eliminate it.

▮ TRY IT OUT ▮➡ **Use Backsolving to answer the question.**

1 Nadia writes the number sentences below.

`3.N.7`

$$4 \times \boxed{} = 4, 10 \times \boxed{} = 10$$

What number belongs in the boxes to make both number sentences correct?

A 0

B 1

C 4

D 10

Try each answer choice to see if it makes the number sentences correct.

• Does (A) make the number sentences correct? _____

• Does (B) make the number sentences correct? _____

• Does (C) make the number sentences correct? _____

• Does (D) make the number sentences correct? _____

All Things Equal

Sometimes, a problem will give you an expression and will ask you to find another way to write it. You can use what you know about number properties and math facts to answer these questions. When you get stuck, you can use All Things Equal to help you identify the best answer.

All Things Equal

- Find the value of the expression in the question.
- Find the value of each answer choice.
- Find the answer choice that has the same value as the expression in the question.

❚ TRY IT OUT ❚ ➡ Use All Things Equal to answer the question.

2 Matthew wrote the expression below in his notebook.

3.N.8

$$17 \times 0$$

Which expression has the same value as Matthew's expression?

A 17×1

B $17 + 0$

C $17 \div 17$

D 0×1

Simplify the expression in the question.

$17 \times 0 = $ _____

Simplify each answer choice.

- Simplify (A): $17 \times 1 = $ _____
- Simplify (C): $17 \div 17 = $ _____

- Simplify (B): $17 + 0 = $ _____
- Simplify (D): $0 \times 1 = $ _____

Find the answer choice that has the same value as the expression in the question.

Independent Practice

Use the 4-Step Method for Problem Solving and the strategies you have learned in this lesson to solve the problems in this section.

1 Margo writes the number sentence below.

3.N.6

$$12 + 3 + 18 = 3 + \boxed{} + 12$$

Which number goes in the empty box to make the number sentence correct?

A 1

B 3

C 12

D 18

hint *Use Backsolving.*

2 Ravi's flower garden is shown below.

3.N.21

Which expression can be used to find the number of flowers in Ravi's garden?

A $5 + 5$

B $3 + 5$

C 3×5

D $5 + 3 + 5$

hint *Use All Things Equal to help you find the answer. Count the number of flowers in the picture and simplify each expression to find the answer.*

3

3.N.7

Ms. Tarbuck wrote this number sentence on the board.

$$11 \times \underline{\hspace{1cm}} = 11$$

What number belongs on the line to make the number sentence correct?

A 0

B 1

C 11

D 12

hint *If you have trouble solving this problem using number properties, use Backsolving.*

4

3.N.6

Koren wrote the expression below.

$$3 \times 2 \times 4$$

Which expression has the same value as the expression Koren wrote?

A $3 + 2 + 4$

B $4 + 2 \times 3$

C $3 \times 3 \times 3$

D $2 \times 4 \times 3$

hint *Simplifying the expressions will make this problem easier to solve.*

5

3.N.18

Melvin wrote the number sentence below.

$$730 - 335 = \boxed{}$$

Which number belongs in the box to make the number sentence correct?

A 305

B 395

C 405

D 495

hint *You can estimate to eliminate wrong answer choices.*

6 Luis writes the number sentence below.

3.N.8

$$4 \times \underline{\hspace{1cm}} = 0$$

What number belongs on the line to make the number sentence correct?

A 0

B 1

C 2

D 4

hint ▷ *Substitute each answer choice for the empty line to find out if it makes the number sentence correct.*

7 Franklin had 24 pictures to use for a computer slide show. He put half of the pictures on his computer. How many pictures has he not yet put on his computer?

3.N.23

A 22

B 20

C 12

D 2

hint ▷ *Start by looking for the total and labeling it on a part-total bar.*

8 Francina wrote the expression below on the board.

3.N.7

$$32 \times 1$$

Which expression has the same value as the expression Francina wrote?

A $32 + 0$

B $32 + 1$

C 32×0

D $32 - 1$

hint *What do you know about the numbers Francina used?*

9 Which of the number sentences below is **not** correct?

3.N.6

A $10 + 6 = 6 + 10$

B $9 \times 2 = 2 \times 9$

C $1 + 4 + 3 = 4 + 1 + 3$

D $7 - 5 = 5 - 7$

hint *Simplify each expression to answer the question.*

10 Jamal wrote the number sentence below.

3.N.22

$$45 \div 9 = \boxed{}$$

Which number belongs in the box to make the number sentence correct?

A 5

B 6

C 7

D 9

hint *Try each answer choice, and see which one works.*

KAP Wrap

Read the question and sample student answer below. Then, use the rubric on page 37 to score the student's work.

1 Julian used shapes to write the number sentence below.

`3.N.6`

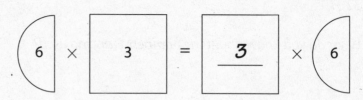

Write one number in the blank shape above to make Julian's number sentence correct.

Julian wrote another number sentence below. Complete the number sentence by writing the correct numbers on the empty lines.

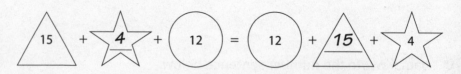

I would give this student a _____ out of 2, because _____

_____

_____

_____

3 Lesson 3
COMPUTATION AND CHECKING

Focus Question

What strategies can you use to check computations?

Thinking KAP

Raheem bought a bag of popcorn for $4. He paid with a $10 bill, and received $5 in change.

Did Raheem receive the right amount of change? How do you know?

_____

_____

_____

_____

Instruction

Checking for Reasonableness

You can use your part-total bar to help you to answer the question, "Is your answer reasonable?" After you solve the problem, return to the part-total bar and use your answer to fill in the missing information.

TRY IT OUT ➡ **Determine whether the student's answer is reasonable.**

1 Sean had 85 blocks. His sister had 62 blocks. How many **more** blocks did Sean have than his sister?

`3.N.18`

    A 11

    B 13

    C 23

    (D) 47

Kya made the part-total bar below and decided to subtract.

> **Write Kya's answer in the part-total bar to make sure it is reasonable.**

85 blocks

? blocks

62 blocks

What expression could Kya use to solve this problem?

When she finished her computation, Kya chose (D). Is Kya's answer reasonable? Why or why not?

_____

_____

_____

Using Inverse Operations

It's easy to make a careless mistake when solving a math problem. You can work backward to check your work. Using a part-total bar can help you keep track of the information in the problem. The part-total bar will tell you how to check your answer.

Addition and Subtraction

When you add, you can check your work by subtracting. When you subtract, you can check your work by adding.

$$
\begin{array}{r} 4\overset{1}{4}8 \\ +104 \\ \hline 552 \end{array}
\qquad
\begin{array}{r} 552 \\ -104 \\ \hline 448 \end{array}
$$

448	104	552

Multiplication and Division

When you multiply, you can check your work by dividing. When you divide, you can check your work by multiplying.

$$
\begin{array}{r} 4 \\ \times 6 \\ \hline 24 \end{array}
\qquad
6\overline{)24}
\begin{array}{r} 4 \\ -24 \\ \hline 0 \end{array}
$$

4	4	4	4	4	4	24

▌TRY IT OUT▐ ➡ **Solve each of the problems below. Then, use inverse operations to check your answers.**

Solve the Problem   **Check Your Work**

2. $\begin{array}{r} 375 \\ +271 \\ \hline \end{array}$

3. $\begin{array}{r} 892 \\ -84 \\ \hline \end{array}$

4. $\begin{array}{r} 3 \\ \times 6 \\ \hline \end{array}$

5. $5\overline{)20}$

Estimate to Check

You can also check your answer by estimating. First, round each number to the highest place value. Then, add, subtract, multiply, or divide the rounded numbers. If your estimated answer is not close to your actual answer, you may have made a mistake.

❚ TRY IT OUT ❚ ➡ **Solve the problem. Then, estimate to check.**

2 On Monday, a fruit stand sold 31 bananas, 18 oranges, and
3.N.18 63 apples. How many pieces of fruit, in total, were sold at the fruit stand on Monday?

Show your work.

Complete the part-total bar to determine how to solve the problem.

_____	_____	_____

Solve the problem in the space below.

Round each of the numbers to the largest place, and estimate to check.

Is your answer reasonable? How do you know?

_____

_____

_____

Estimate to Solve

Some problems will ask you to find the best estimate, rather than to identify an exact number. You must estimate to solve these problems, and should do so just as you estimate to check.

Round the numbers before you calculate to determine the best estimate. You can even put the rounded numbers into a part-total bar, instead of the exact numbers.

∎ TRY IT OUT ∎ ➡ **Round and compute to find the best estimate.**

3 Sohalia biked 286 yards on Monday, 404 yards on Tuesday,
3.N.25 and 191 yards on Wednesday. What is the **best estimate** of the number of yards Sohalia biked during those three days?

- **A** 700
- **B** 800
- **C** 900
- **D** 1,000

Identify the important information in the problem. Then, round the numbers and use the rounded numbers to complete a part-total bar.

What operation can you use to find the best estimate? _____

In the space below, calculate and find the best estimate. Then, select the correct answer choice above.

Independent Practice

Use the 4-Step Method for Problem Solving and the strategies you have learned in this lesson to solve the problems in this section.

1

3.N.25

Diego and his family went on a trip. They drove 142 kilometers to visit his grandmother. They then drove 368 kilometers to visit his sister at college and 309 kilometers to get back home. What is the **best estimate** of the total number of kilometers Diego's family drove?

A 700

B 800

C 900

D 1,000

hint *Underline the clue words that tell you what the problem is asking you to find.*

2

3.N.22

There are 56 mice in 8 burrows. There are an equal number of mice in each burrow. How many mice are in each burrow?

A 5

B 6

C 7

D 8

hint *Solve the problem. Then, use inverse operations to check your solution.*

3

3.N.18

Cavender Lane is 192 feet long. Murphy Road is 480 feet long. How much longer is Murphy Road than Cavender Lane?

A 288

B 298

C 312

D 391

hint *What operation should you use? What inverse operation will help you check your answer?*

4 The drawing below shows the number of students participating in each of three after-school activities in a large school district.

3.N.25

Band ♪	Drama Club 🎭	Debate Team 👄
205	178	56

Which is the **best estimate** of the total number of students who participate in the after-school activities?

A 300

B 400

C 500

D 600

hint ▷ *Use the information from the picture to help you answer the question.*

5 Kenji wants to estimate the sum of the numbers below.

3.N.25

$$48 + 73 + 44$$

Which is the best way for Kenji to **estimate** the sum?

A $40 + 70 + 40$

B $50 + 70 + 40$

C $40 + 80 + 50$

D $50 + 80 + 50$

hint ▷ *Use a place-value chart to help you round each number.*

6

3.N.19

Sheldon has 9 packs of markers. There are 7 markers in each pack. How many markers does Sheldon have?

A 2

B 8

C 16

D 63

hint *Make a part-total bar. After you solve the problem, put your solution into the part-total bar to check if it is reasonable.*

7

3.N.20

Kelly made 6 trips from her apartment to the store last week. The distance from Kelly's apartment to the store and back is 12 blocks. What is the total number of blocks Kelly traveled to the store and back last week?

A 2

B 6

C 18

D 72

hint *Draw a diagram to help you solve the problem.*

8

3.N.18

Marisa's family recycled 29 cans in January and 57 cans in February. How many total cans did the family recycle during the first two months of the year?

A 76

B 86

C 88

D 92

hint *What strategy can you use to check your work?*

9

3.N.25
3.N.26

Elton wants to buy 4 shirts. The shirts cost $19, $17, $23, and $32.

Elton has $80. **Estimate** the total cost of the shirts. Does Elton have enough money to buy all the shirts?

Show your work.

Answer _____

On the lines below, explain why you were able to estimate instead of finding the exact answer to determine whether Elton had enough money.

_____

_____

_____

_____

hint ▷ *Use rounded numbers in a part-total bar to estimate the answer.*

KAP Wrap

Read the question and sample student answer below. Then, use the rubric on page 37 to score the student's work.

1

3.N.25

Vera is making a necklace out of tiny beads. She uses 28 blue beads, 71 yellow beads, 46 pink beads, and 13 green beads. Write the number sentence that Vera can use to estimate the total number of beads in her necklace.

Show your work.

28	30
71	80
46	50
13	20

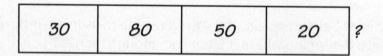

30	80	50	20	?

Expression ___30 + 80 + 50 + 20___

I would give this student a _____ out of 2, because _____

_____

_____

_____

UNIT 4 Strategies for Statistics and Probability

I USE BAR GRAPHS TO HELP MY TEAM MAKE DECISIONS.

EXECUTIVE

1

Lesson 1
PICTOGRAPHS

Focus Question
   How does a pictograph show information?

Thinking KAP

Shar wants to knit toys for the cats in her apartment building. She draws the picture of her building below.

Complete the pictograph below by drawing one cat symbol for each of the cats owned by Shar's neighbors.

APARTMENT BUILDING CATS

Neighbor	Number of Cats Owned
Mr. Crothers	
Dr. Nile	
Jenkins Family	
Mr. and Mrs. West	

KEY
🐱 = 1 cat

Reading Pictographs

A **pictograph** shows data, or information. On the Math Test, you will answer questions about pictographs.

When you read a pictograph, pay careful attention to three types of clues:

Words, Numbers, Shape (for Pictographs)	
• **Words**	Read the title, column headings, and entries.
• **Numbers**	Look at the key.
• **Shape**	Look at the icons.

Words
The title, column headings, and entries tell you what the graph shows.

Numbers
The key tells you what each icon represents.

Shape
The icons show the data for each row.

KEN'S MILEAGE

Day	Number of Miles Driven
Monday	🚗 🚗 🚗
Tuesday	🚗 🚗
Wednesday	🚗 🚗 🚗

KEY
🚗 = 5 miles

The Key

On the Math Test, icons in pictographs will almost always represent more than one item. Don't forget to look at the key!

In the pictograph above, how many miles does each car icon represent?

Mark It

Words, Numbers, Shape will help you find the information you need to answer questions about a pictograph. Once you find the information you need, mark it on the graph. If you need only one of the rows in the graph, label that row and ignore the others.

▌TRY IT OUT▐ ➡ **Use Words, Numbers, Shape to answer the problem about the pictograph below. Mark information on the graph to help you.**

1 The number of bicycles sold at a store during a 3-month period is shown on the pictograph below.

3.S.7

BICYCLES SOLD

Month	Number of Bicycles
June	🚲🚲🚲🚲
July	🚲🚲🚲
August	🚲🚲🚲🚲🚲

KEY
🚲 = 2 bicycles

How many **more** bicycles were sold in August than in July?

A 2

B 3

C 4

D 5

- Use the key to figure out the number of bicycles sold in August. Mark the number sold next to the August row.

- Use the key to figure out the number of bicycles sold in July. Mark the number sold next to the July row.

- Compare the numbers next to the two rows.

Making Pictographs

On the Math Test, you may be asked to complete unfinished pictographs. Use the strategy below to make sure you draw in the correct number of icons in each row.

Count By the Key

- Look at the key.
- Look at the number of items you want to show.
- Draw icons, counting by the key each time, until you reach the number you want to show.

▌TRY IT OUT▐ ➡ **Count by the key to complete each pictograph below.**

Complete the pictograph below to show that the soccer team scored 8 goals in Game 1. Be sure to use the key provided.

SOCCER GOALS

Game	Number of Goals Scored
1	

KEY
⚽ = 2 goals

Complete the pictograph below to show that Teresa inflated 25 balloons. Be sure to use the key provided.

BALLOONS INFLATED

Name	Number of Balloons Inflated
Teresa	

KEY
🎈 = 5 balloons

Complete the pictograph below to show that Steve swam 35 laps on Monday. Be sure to use the key provided.

STEVE'S SWIMMING

Day	Number of Laps
Monday	

KEY
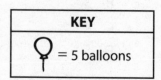 = 10 laps

2

3.5.5

Ms. Ellis sells bagels. Yesterday, she sold 20 wheat bagels, 30 cheese bagels, 50 sesame-seed bagels, and 80 blueberry bagels.

Complete the pictograph below to show all the bagels Ms. Ellis sold yesterday. Be sure to use the key provided.

YESTERDAY'S BAGEL SALES

Type of Bagel	Number of Bagels
Wheat	
Cheese	
Sesame Seed	
Blueberry	

KEY
◯ = 10 bagels

Ms. Ellis also sold 45 onion bagels yesterday. If she adds a row to her pictograph for onion bagels, how many icons should she draw in the row?

Answer _____ icons

On the lines below, explain how you figured out the number of icons Ms. Ellis should draw to show her onion-bagel sales.

_____

_____

_____

UNIT 4 ● ②

Independent Practice

Use the 4-Step Method for Problem Solving and the strategies you have learned in this lesson to solve the problems in this section.

1 The number of hours Tristan spent reading with his sister Louise over a 4-month period is
3.5.7 shown on the pictograph below.

READING WITH LOUISE

Month	Number of Hours
January	🕐 🕐
February	🕐 🕐 🕐
March	🕐 🕐 🕐 🕐
April	🕐 🕐 🕐

KEY
🕐 = 5 hours

How many hours did Tristan spend reading with Louise in March?

A 3

B 4

C 15

D 20

hint ▶ *Use Words, Numbers, Shape to understand the pictograph and its key.*

2

3.S.7

The pictograph below shows the number of flags flying on Washington Street on four different holidays.

FLAGS FLYING ON WASHINGTON STREET

Holiday	Number of Flags
Presidents' Day	🏴 🏴 🏴
Memorial Day	🏴 🏴 🏴
Flag Day	🏴 🏴 🏴 🏴
Fourth of July	🏴 🏴 🏴 🏴 🏴

KEY
🏴 = 2 flags

How many **more** flags were flying on Washington Street on the Fourth of July than on Memorial Day?

A 2

B 3

C 4

D 5

hint ▷ *Mark information on the graph that will help you solve the problem.*

3

3.5.5
3.5.7

Chandre's family went apple picking last Saturday. The table below shows the number of apples picked by each member of her family.

SATURDAY APPLE PICKING

Family Member	Number of Apples Picked
Chandre	20
Derek	10
Mom	40
Dad	30
Uncle Wes	60

How many **more** apples did Uncle Wes pick than Derek?

Show your work.

Answer _____ apples

What is the total number of apples picked by members of Chandre's family?

Show your work.

Answer _____ apples

Complete the pictograph below to show all the apples that members of Chandre's family picked last Saturday. Be sure to use the key provided.

SATURDAY APPLE PICKING

Family Member	Number of Apples Picked
Chandre	
Derek	
Mom	
Dad	
Uncle Wes	

KEY
= 10 apples

hint ▷ *Count By the Key to make sure you draw the correct number of apple icons in each row.*

KAP Wrap

Read the question and sample student answer below. Then, use the rubric on page 37 to score the student's work.

1 Ryan does the laundry for his family. In the past month, he washed 5 loads of laundry in hot water, 5 loads of laundry in warm water, and 10 loads of laundry in cold water.

3.S.5

Complete the pictograph below to show all the loads of laundry Ryan washed last month. Be sure to use the key provided.

RYAN'S LAUNDRY LOADS

Type of Water Used	Number of Loads Washed
Hot	👕👕👕👕👕
Warm	👕👕👕👕👕
Cold	👕👕👕👕👕👕👕👕👕👕

KEY
👕 = 5 loads

I would give this student a _____ out of 2, because _____

_____

_____

_____

Lesson 2
BAR GRAPHS

Focus Question
  How does a bar graph show information?

Thinking KAP

Four students in Mrs. Beeker's class have been collecting shoe boxes for the class mail system. Evan has collected 5 boxes, Cindy has collected 2 boxes, Monique has collected 4 boxes, and Daryl has collected 1 box.

Evan and Cindy made a bar graph to keep track of this data. They each drew a stack of boxes to show the number of boxes they had collected.

Help Monique and Daryl by drawing stacks of boxes on the graph to show the number of shoe boxes each of them has collected.

Reading Bar Graphs

A **bar graph** shows data, or information. On the Math Test, you will answer questions about bar graphs.

When you read a bar graph, pay careful attention to three types of clues:

Words, Numbers, Shape (for Bar Graphs)

- **Words**   Read the title and labels.
- **Numbers**   Look at the scale.
- **Shape**   Look at the height of the bars.

Words
The title and axis labels tell you what the graph shows.

Numbers
The scale tells you what amount each bar stands for.

Shape
Shaded bars show how many of each item there are.

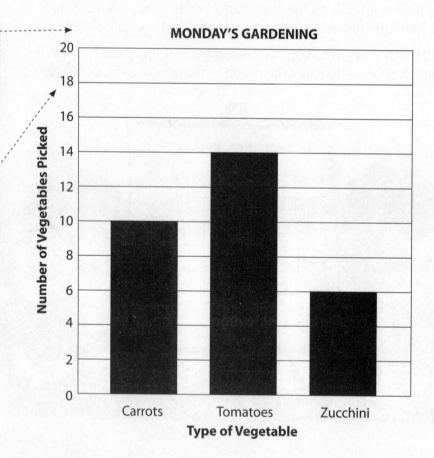

The Scale

On the Math Test, the scale of each bar graph may be different. It may count by ones, twos, fives, or tens. Don't forget to look at the scale!

In the bar graph above, what number does the scale count by? _____

Mark It

Words, Numbers, Shape will help you find the information you need to answer questions about a bar graph. Once you find the information you need, mark it on the graph. If you need only one of the bars in the graph, label that bar and ignore the others.

❚ TRY IT OUT ❚➡ **Use Words, Numbers, Shape to answer the question about the bar graph below.**

1 The bar graph below shows the amount of money four students earned in one week.

`3.5.7`

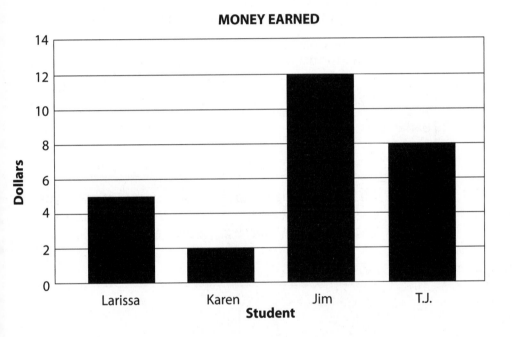

How much **more** money did Jim earn than Karen?

A $2

B $5

C $10

D $12

- Use the scale to figure out how much money Karen earned. Mark the amount above the bar that represents her earnings.

- Use the scale to figure out how much money Jim earned. Mark the amount above the bar that represents his earnings.

- Compare the numbers above the two bars.

Making Bar Graphs

On the Math Test, you may be asked to complete unfinished bar graphs. Data that is organized in a table can be put into a bar graph.

TRY IT OUT ➡ **Use Words, Numbers, Shape to move data from the table to the bar graph.**

2

3.S.5

Students in classroom 6 sold fruit smoothies on Friday. The table below shows the type and number of smoothies they sold.

FRIDAY'S SMOOTHIE SALES

Type of Smoothie	Number of Smoothies Sold
Strawberry	10
Banana	20
Orange	15

Complete the bar graph below to show the number of each type of smoothie the students in classroom 6 sold on Friday. Be sure to fill in all blanks, finish numbering the scale, and graph any missing data.

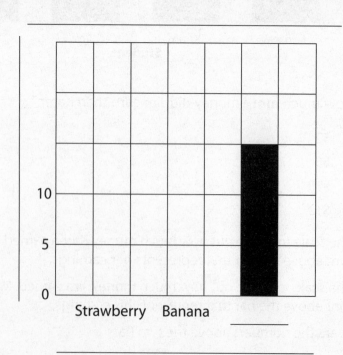

❚ TRY IT OUT ❚➡ Use Words, Numbers, Shape to complete the bar graph.

3

3.5.5

Sarah is studying birds for a school project. The table below shows the type and number of birds she observed in the schoolyard on Friday at lunchtime.

BIRDS OBSERVED ON FRIDAY AT LUNCHTIME

Type of Bird	Number of Birds Observed
Robin	4
Sparrow	8
Cardinal	7

Words
This is the title of the table and the graph.

Words
Use the column headings to label the axes.

Complete the bar graph below to show the number of each type of bird Sarah observed on Friday at lunchtime.

Be sure to
• label the blank axis
• graph all data

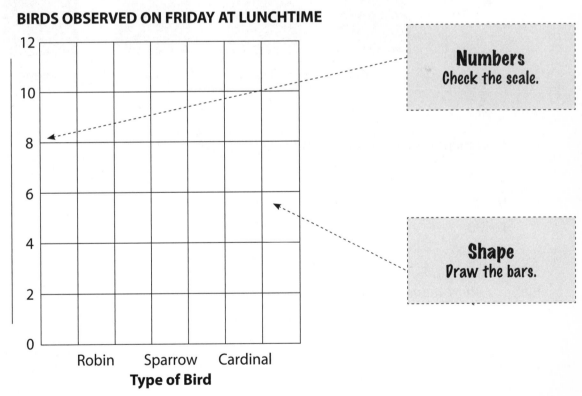

BIRDS OBSERVED ON FRIDAY AT LUNCHTIME

Numbers
Check the scale.

Shape
Draw the bars.

UNIT 4 ①

Independent Practice

Use the 4-Step Method for Problem Solving and the strategies you have learned in this lesson to solve the problems in this section.

1 The bar graph below shows the number of e-mails Susan, Edward, Miles, and Selena each sent in one week.

3.S.7

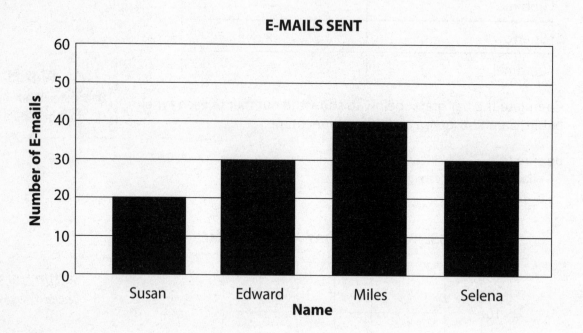

E-MAILS SENT

How many e-mails did Susan and Selena send in total?

A 10

B 20

C 30

D 50

hint ▷ *Above the appropriate bars, mark the number of e-mails that Susan and Selena each sent.*

2 The bar graph below shows the number of books four students read in one week.

3.5.7

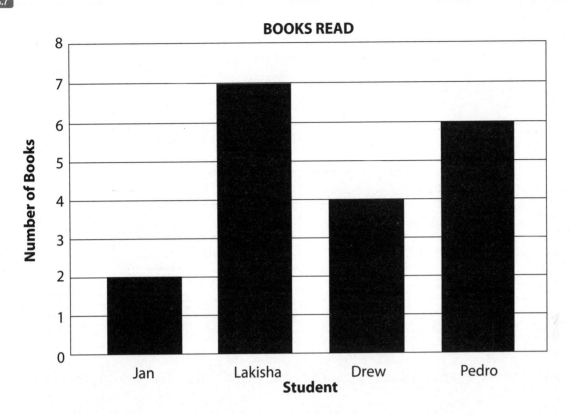

Who read the **most** books?

Answer _____

How many **more** books must Jan read to have read the same number of books as Pedro?

Show your work.

Answer _____ books

hint ▶ *Use the shape of the bars to help you answer the first question.*

3

3.5.5

Lucy is practicing a speech she will give to her class. The table below shows the number of times she practiced her speech for each day of the school week

LUCY'S SPEECH PRACTICE

Day	Number of Times Practiced
Monday	4
Tuesday	4
Wednesday	6
Thursday	10
Friday	8

How many **more** times did Lucy practice her speech on Thursday than on Tuesday?

Show your work.

Answer _____ times

What is the total number of times Lucy practiced her speech Monday through Friday?

Show your work.

Answer _____ times

Complete the bar graph below to show the number of times Lucy practiced her speech on each day of the school week.

Be sure to
- label the blank axis
- graph all the data

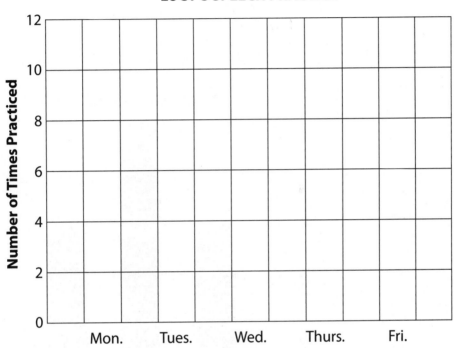

LUCY'S SPEECH PRACTICE

Number of Times Practiced

12

10

8

6

4

2

0

Mon.   Tues.   Wed.   Thurs.   Fri.

_____

hint ▷ _Read the words in the table to help you figure out how to label the blank axis._

UNIT 4

KAP Wrap

Read the question and sample student answer below. Then, use the rubric on page 37 to score the student's work.

1

3.5.5

Ryan is collecting leaves for an art project. He has collected 4 elm leaves, 6 maple leaves, and 4 oak leaves.

Complete the bar graph below to show the number of each type of leaf Ryan has collected. Be sure to label the blank axis.

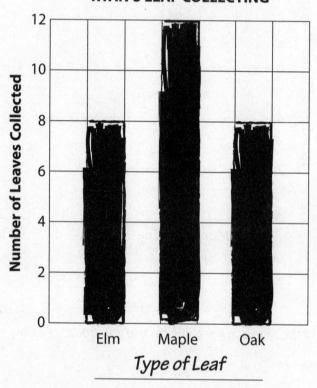

RYAN'S LEAF COLLECTING

I would give this student a _____ out of 2, because _____

_____

_____

_____

Mini Practice Test 2

Mini Practice Test 2

1.	Ⓐ	Ⓑ	Ⓒ	Ⓓ	**5.**	Ⓐ	Ⓑ	Ⓒ	Ⓓ	**9.**	Ⓐ	Ⓑ	Ⓒ	Ⓓ
2.	Ⓐ	Ⓑ	Ⓒ	Ⓓ	**6.**	Ⓐ	Ⓑ	Ⓒ	Ⓓ	**10.**	Ⓐ	Ⓑ	Ⓒ	Ⓓ
3.	Ⓐ	Ⓑ	Ⓒ	Ⓓ	**7.**	Ⓐ	Ⓑ	Ⓒ	Ⓓ	**11.**	Ⓐ	Ⓑ	Ⓒ	Ⓓ
4.	Ⓐ	Ⓑ	Ⓒ	Ⓓ	**8.**	Ⓐ	Ⓑ	Ⓒ	Ⓓ	**12.**	Ⓐ	Ⓑ	Ⓒ	Ⓓ

Your answers for questions 13–14 should be written in the test booklet.

1 The pictograph below shows the number of computers sold over 4 weeks.

COMPUTERS SOLD

Week	Number of Computers
Week 1	
Week 2	
Week 3	
Week 4	

KEY
= 3 computers

How many **more** computers were sold in Week 3 than Week 2?

A 2

B 3

C 6

D 9

2 Joo-Yun wants to estimate the sum of the numbers below.

687 + 217 + 394

Which way is best for Joo-Yun to estimate the sum?

A 600 + 200 + 300

B 600 + 200 + 400

C 700 + 200 + 400

D 700 + 300 + 400

Go On

3 Jenny skipped rope 187 times. George skipped rope 205 times. How many times did Jenny and George skip rope all together?

A 18

B 89

C 392

D 412

4 Karstein saved the amount of money shown below.

How much money did Karstein save?

A $2.06

B $2.38

C $2.48

D $2.53

5 Rowena planted 8 rows of vegetable seeds in her garden. Each row had 6 seeds. How many vegetable seeds did Rowena plant in all?

A 2

B 14

C 36

D 48

6 Selma has teacups lined up on her kitchen shelf.

Which expression can be used to find the number of teacups on Selma's shelf?

A 3 + 4
B 4 − 3
C 3 + 3 + 3
D 3 × 4

7 Frances spent the coins shown below to buy a carton of milk at school.

How much did Frances pay for the milk?

A $0.12
B $0.78
C $0.87
D $1.02

Go On

8 The bar graph below shows the ways students get to Lyle School in the morning.

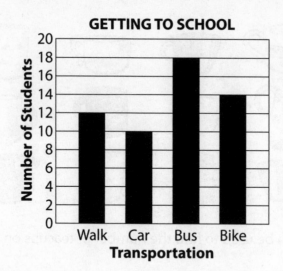

GETTING TO SCHOOL

How many **more** students take the bus than walk to school?

A 3 students

B 6 students

C 12 students

D 30 students

9 Carey's class has an even number of students. Which number could be the number of students in Carey's class?

A 23

B 25

C 28

D 29

10 Bijal has 12 posters to put up in her room. She put the same number of posters on each of her 4 walls. How many posters are on each wall if Bijal put up all of her posters?

A 2

B 3

C 8

D 48

11 The bar graph below shows the number of students who participated in a service drive in each grade.

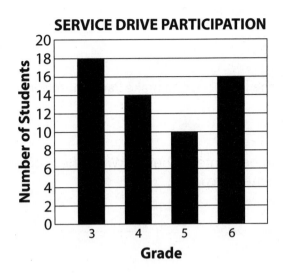

How many students in grades 4 and 5 participated, in all?

A 4

B 14

C 24

D 30

12 Belinda put all of her books on 6 shelves. She put 9 books on each shelf. How many books does Belinda have?

A 3

B 9

C 15

D 54

Go On

13 Paul writes the number sentence below.

$$7 + 3 = 3 + \underline{\hspace{2cm}}$$

Write one number on the line above to make Paul's number sentence correct.

Paul writes another number sentence below. Write one number on each of the lines below to make this number sentence correct.

$$\underline{\hspace{2cm}} + 4 = 4 + \underline{\hspace{2cm}}$$

KAPLAN ADVANTAGE
NEW YORK MATHEMATICS GRADE 3

14 Deidre took a survey of her classmates to find out which sport they liked best. Her results are shown in the table below.

FAVORITE SPORTS

Sport	Number of Students
Basketball	8
Hockey	7
Track	3
Volleyball	5

How many students answered Deidre's survey in all?

Answer _____ students

Complete the bar graph below to show the number of students who voted for each sport.

Be sure to
- label the blank axis
- graph all the data

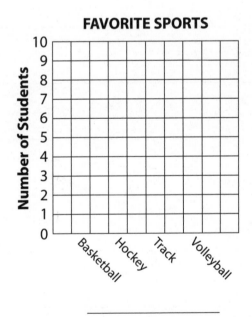

FAVORITE SPORTS

STOP

Reflection

Reflect on your work on the Mini Practice Test by completing the table below. First, rate each question by circling either "comfortable" or "challenging." Then, under the "How did you figure out the answer?" column, write the name of the strategy you used to answer each question.

Question	Rate this question!	How did you figure out the answer?
1	Comfortable Challenging	
2	Comfortable Challenging	
3	Comfortable Challenging	
4	Comfortable Challenging	
5	Comfortable Challenging	
6	Comfortable Challenging	
7	Comfortable Challenging	
8	Comfortable Challenging	
9	Comfortable Challenging	
10	Comfortable Challenging	
11	Comfortable Challenging	
12	Comfortable Challenging	

Reflect on Open-Ended Problems

For each problem you got right, describe what really helped you to solve the problem.

- Did you read carefully?

- Did you check your work?

- Did you think back to mistakes you had made before and avoid them?

For each problem you got wrong, describe the error that you made. Based on your answers, give yourself some advice for Test Day.

Question	What did you do to solve the problem that really helped you? or What error did you make?	What advice do you have for yourself on Test Day?
13		
14		

UNIT 5 Strategies for Geometry and Measurement

I USE BASIC SHAPES TO SKETCH MY CHARACTERS.

CARTOONIST

1 Lesson 1
SHAPES AND SOLIDS

Focus Question
   What vocabulary do you need to know to answer problems about shapes and solids?

Thinking KAP

Cathy drew a picture of the playground in the park.

List all the shapes you can find in Cathy's picture.

_____

_____

Instruction

Polygons

A **polygon** is a closed figure that has three or more sides. You can count the number of sides to find the name of the shape. Here are two polygons you should know:

Polygon	Draw one that is...	Draw one that is not...
A **triangle** has 3 sides, just like a tricycle has 3 wheels.		
A **hexagon** has 6 sides. The word "hexagon" and the word "six" both have an "x" in them.		

A **quadrilateral** is any polygon with 4 sides. Make sure you know these special names for quadrilaterals.

Quadrilateral	Draw one that is...	Draw one that is not...
A **trapezoid** has 1 pair of parallel sides.		
A **rectangle** has 2 pairs of opposite sides that are the same length, and 4 square corners.		
A **square** has 4 sides that are all the same length, and 4 square corners.		
A **rhombus** has 4 sides that are all the same length.		

KAPLAN ADVANTAGE
NEW YORK MATHEMATICS GRADE 3

Lines of Symmetry

A figure has **symmetry** if it can be folded in half so that the two halves match exactly. The figure is folded over a **line of symmetry**. A figure can have no lines of symmetry, one line of symmetry, or many lines of symmetry. Look at the examples below.

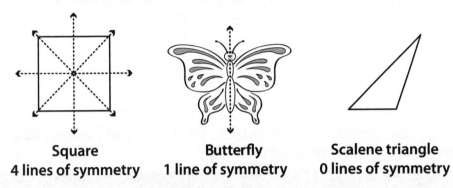

Square	Butterfly	Scalene triangle
4 lines of symmetry	**1 line of symmetry**	**0 lines of symmetry**

Think of a line of symmetry as a mirror. Whatever is on one side of the mirror is exactly like the image on the other side, just reversed. To find out if a figure has a line of symmetry, draw a line and match the two sides.

▌TRY IT OUT▌➡   **Solve the problem below.**

1   Which shape below has a line of symmetry?

`3.G.5`

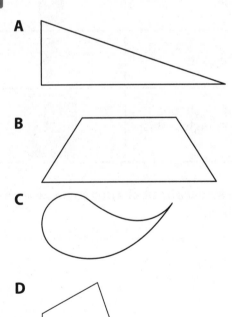

A

B

C

D

Draw lines through each figure to find if the two sides match.

UNIT 5

Real-World Solids

A three-dimensional **solid** is made up of two-dimensional **faces**.

face

Three-dimensional solids are like objects you see around you every day. Here are a few solids you should know.

Solid	Real-World Example
A cube has 6 sides that are all squares. A block is an example of a cube.	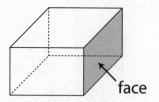
A globe is an example of a sphere.	
A soup can is an example of a cylinder.	
An ice-cream cone is an example of a cone.	
A prism is any figure that has 2 polygon-shaped bases and other faces that are all rectangles. This cereal box is a prism.	

▌TRY IT OUT▐ ➡ **Use what you know about shapes to answer the questions below.**

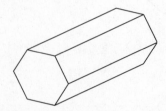

How many faces does the figure have? _____

What shapes are the faces? _____

Congruent and Similar Shapes

Shapes are **congruent** if they have the same shape and size. You can think of *congruent* shapes as exact copies of each other—even if one is turned.

Shapes are **similar** if they have the same shape but not necessarily the same size. Think of *similar* shapes as if you made a copy but scaled the copy up or down.

I TRY IT OUT I ➡ **In each row of the table below, draw a shape that is similar to the given shape.**

Shape	Similar Shape

Independent Practice

Use the 4-Step Method for Problem Solving and the strategies you have learned in this lesson to solve the problems in this section.

1 Maxine drew the figure below.

Which of the following is congruent to Maxine's figure?

A

B

C

D

> **hint** *Imagine turning the figure in your head to see if it is congruent.*

2 What is the shape of the traffic symbol shown below?

A cone

B cube

C cylinder

D sphere

> **hint** *What other real-world objects does the traffic symbol look like?*

3 Which shape has a line of symmetry?

3.6.5

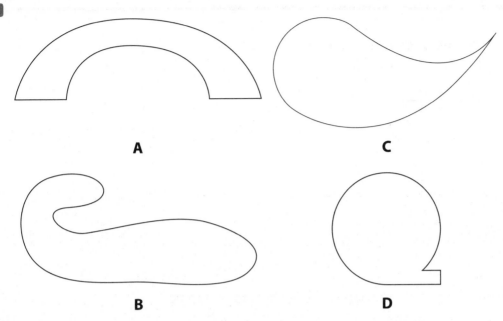

A

C

B

D

hint *Could you draw a line that divides the shape into mirror images?*

4 Which figure could be one face of this box?

3.6.4

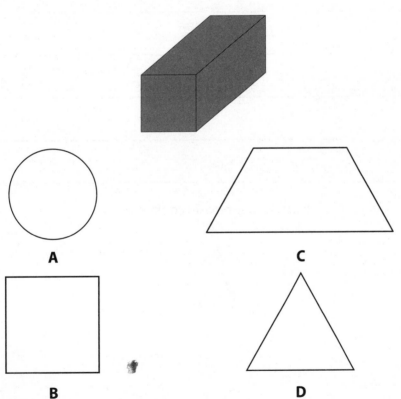

A

C

B

D

hint *Which shape matches one of the faces of the box?*

5 Naomi drew the five shapes shown below.

3.G.1

Draw a ring around all of the shapes above that are rectangles.

On the lines below, write two things that all rectangles have in common.

_____

_____

_____

_____

_____

hint ▷ *Look at the rectangles. What do they have in common?*

6 Hector drew the two rows of shapes shown below.

3.6.1

3.6.5

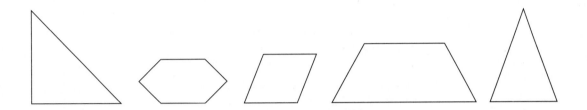

Draw a ring around the trapezoid that is **next to** a rhombus in the rows of shapes above.

Draw one line of symmetry on the rectangle above.

hint ▷ *Read the problem carefully to find which shape to draw a ring around.*

KAP Wrap

Read the problem and sample student answer below. Then, use the rubric on page 37 to score the student's work.

1 Jelanie is comparing many different squares.

3.6.1

Draw 2 squares on the grid below. Make one square larger than the other.

On the lines below, tell Jelanie one way that all squares are alike.

They all have 4 sides and 4 square corners.

I would give this student a _____ out of 2, because _____

Lesson 2
TIME AND MONEY

Focus Question

What strategies can you use to solve time and money problems?

Thinking KAP

Jeremy had the following coins in his pocket.

Write the name of each coin Jeremy has beside each picture.

Measuring Money

You know that when you get change from a dollar, you get pennies, nickels, dimes, and quarters. You should know how to write the value of each coin using the dollar symbol and a decimal point.

Coin	Value	Using a Dollar Symbol
	1 cent	$0.01

▌TRY IT OUT▐ ➤ **Use what you know about coins to solve the problem below.**

Draw coins below that have a total value of $0.36.

Grouping

To measure money in math problems, group the dollars and cents into easy-to-count groups.

Grouping
• Group the whole dollars.
• Count the loose change in easy groups.

To group the loose change, use groups that make sense. For example, if there are 2 quarters, a group of 50 cents makes it easy to count. If there are several dimes, groups of 10 make sense.

▌TRY IT OUT▐ ➧ **Solve the problem below.**

1

3.M.7

Sheri has the money shown below in her pocket. How much money is shown?

A $0.55

B $0.85

C $1.15

D $1.55

Which answer choices can you eliminate? _____

How can you group the coins? _____

_____

Telling Time

Some problems will ask you to measure time using different types of clocks. Time can be measured using hours and minutes. Whenever you see a clock, find the time by looking at the hours and minutes.

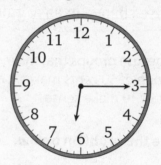

First, find the hour. When the hour hand (the shorter hand) is between 6 and 7, that means it is past 6:00 but not yet 7:00. So, write 6 as the hour.

Next, use the minute hand (the longer hand) to find the number of minutes. You can skip-count by 5s to check that you found the correct number of minutes.

▌TRY IT OUT▐▶ **Draw hands on the clock to show each time.**

1. 4:50

2. 8:10

Fractions and Time

You can use fractions to help you solve problems about time as well. In everyday life, you hear people say, "It's half past 5" or "It's a quarter to 2." Think about the face of a clock, and divide it into halves or quarters.

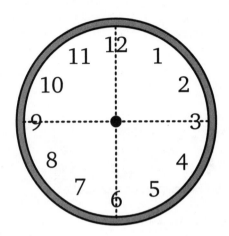

Half of an hour equals 30 minutes, and a quarter of an hour equals 15 minutes.

▌TRY IT OUT▌ ➡ **Use what you know about fractions to help you find the time.**

2 What time will it be when $\frac{1}{2}$ of an hour has passed?

`3.A.1`

A 5:15

B 5:30

C 5:45

D 6:30

Divide the clock into halves to find the answer.

UNIT 5

Independent Practice

Use the 4-Step Method for Problem Solving and the strategies you have learned in this lesson to solve the problems in this section.

1 The clock below shows the time Rita woke up this morning.

3.M.9

Which clock below shows the time that Rita woke up?

A

C

B

D

hint ▷   *Look at the hours and minutes to find the right clock.*

2 After buying a CD, Rick has this much money left.

3.M.7

How much money does Rick have left?

A $2.40

B $2.50

C $2.75

D $2.85

hint *Use Grouping to find the total amount.*

3 What time will it be when $\frac{1}{4}$ of an hour has passed from the time shown on the clock below?

3.M.8

A 4:15

B 4:30

C 4:45

D 5:15

hint *Divide the clock into quarters.*

UNIT 5

4 Janelle spends $0.46 to buy a piece of fruit. Which group of coins shows exactly $0.46?

3.M.7

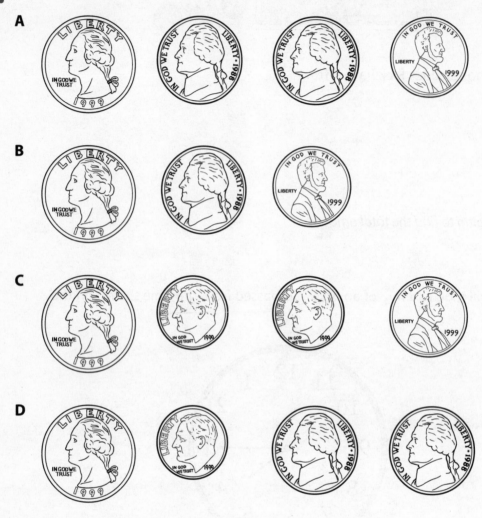

A

B

C

D

hint ▷ *Which answer choices can you eliminate?*

5 What is the time on the clock below?

3.M.9

A 6:03

B 6:12

C 12:06

D 12:30

hint ▷ *Which two numbers is the hour hand between?*

6 What is the time on the clock below?

3.M.9

A 10:03

B 10:15

C 3:10

D 3:50

hint ▷ *What does the minute hand show?*

UNIT 5 ① ● ③ ④

KAP Wrap

Read the problem and sample student answer below. Then, use the rubric on page 37 to score the student's work.

---

1 What is the time on the clock below?

3.M.9

Answer   3:00

Explain how you know what time the clock shows.

The hand pointing to the 3 shows the hour and the hand pointing to the 12 shows the minutes, so it shows 3:00.

I would give this student a _____ out of 2, because _____

_____

_____

_____

3 Lesson 3
MEASURING LENGTH

Focus Question
How can you use a ruler and different units to measure length?

Thinking KAP

Janie drew a picture of the area where she lives and put stars on both ends of her block.

How long, in inches, does the block measure in Janie's picture?

_____

Instruction

Ruler Rules

When you see a picture of a ruler next to a test problem, it means that you will need to use your ruler to measure something.

Ruler Rules
• Locate the inches side of the ruler.
• Line up the edge of the ruler with the object you want to measure.
• Write all of the measurements on the diagram.

Make sure you measure the line next to the picture, and not the picture itself.

▌TRY IT OUT ▌➡ **Solve the problem below.**

1   Use your ruler to help you solve this problem.

3.M.2

Which hair clip measures exactly 2 inches long?

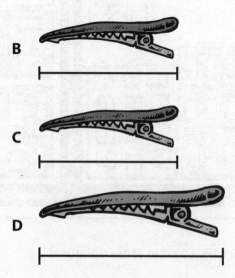

A

B

C

D

Draw It

You may need to use your ruler to draw your own shapes. Follow the Ruler Rules to help you draw the correct shape.

▌TRY IT OUT▌➡ **Solve the problem below.**

2 Use your ruler to help you solve this problem.

3.M.2

Draw a square that is 3 inches long on each side.

Use the Ruler Rules.

- Find the inches side of your ruler and carefully draw a line segment 3 inches long in the space above.

- Complete the other three sides.

- Check your drawing. Are all the sides the same length?

Touchstones for Length

Making a connection between a standard unit of measurement and a familiar object can help you solve measurement problems. You can think of these familiar objects as touchstones.

Touchstone Table for Length

1 inch	about the width of a postage stamp
1 foot	about the length of a piece of paper 1 ft = 12 in.
1 yard	about the length of a baseball bat 1 yd = 3 ft
1 mile	about the distance a person would walk in 15 minutes 1 mile = 5,280 ft

▮TRY IT OUT▮➡ **Use the Touchstone Table to answer the following questions.**

1. Which unit(s) could you use to measure the length of your bedroom?

   _____

2. Which unit(s) could you use to measure the length of a puppy?

   _____

3. Which unit(s) could you use to measure the distance between cities?

   _____

Makeshift Measuring

Sometimes, instead of showing you a picture of a measurement tool, a math problem may ask you to estimate a measurement using another object. For these problems, you can use your fingers to help you estimate.

Makeshift Measuring

- Put two or three fingers together and place them at one end of the object you want to measure.
- Make a small mark on the diagram to show where your fingers end.
- Keep measuring using your fingers and marking the diagram.

TRY IT OUT ➡ **Use Makeshift Measuring to help you solve the problem below.**

3 Tamyra is measuring her pencil using the paper clip shown below.

3.M.10

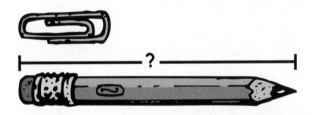

About how many paper clips long is Tamyra's pencil?

A 3 paper clips

B 4 paper clips

C 5 paper clips

D 6 paper clips

Independent Practice

Use the 4-Step Method for Problem Solving and the strategies you have learned in this lesson to solve the problems in this section.

1 Use your ruler to help you solve this problem.

3.M.2

Claire has the doll below.

How many inches tall is the doll?

A $2\frac{1}{2}$

B 3

C $3\frac{1}{2}$

D 4

hint ▷ *Measure the line, not the doll.*

2  Use your ruler to help you solve this problem.

3.M.2

Which stick is closest to 2 inches long?

A

B

C

D

hint ▷ *Measure each choice and mark the diagram.*

3 Which unit of measure is **best** to use for measuring the length of a playing card?

3.M.1

A mile

B yard

C inch

D foot

hint ▷ *Which unit would you use to measure a small object?*

UNIT 5 ① ② ● ④

4 Philip is measuring a postcard using the thumbtack shown below.

3.M.10

About how many thumbtacks long is Philip's postcard?

A 5

B 7

C 9

D 11

hint *Use your fingers to measure the thumbtack and the postcard.*

5 Which unit of measure is **best** to use for measuring the distance between New York and Florida?

3.M.1

A foot

B yard

C inch

D mile

hint *Which unit is used to measure long distances?*

6

3.M.2

Use your ruler to help you solve this problem.

Jason measured the length of the chalkboard eraser shown below.

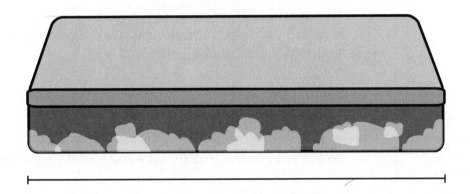

How many inches long is the chalkboard eraser?

A 4

B $4\frac{1}{2}$

C 5

D $5\frac{1}{2}$

hint *Make sure to measure to the nearest $\frac{1}{2}$ inch.*

7 Which unit of measure is **best** to use for measuring the length of a butterfly?

3.M.1

A mile

B foot

C inch

D yard

hint *How big is a butterfly?*

KAP Wrap

Read the problem and sample student answer below. Then, use the rubric on page 37 to score the student's work.

1

3.M.1

Julia is in the third grade. What is the **best estimate** of the length of Julia's hand; 5 inches or 5 feet?

Answer _5 inches_

On the lines below, explain how you found your answer.

It was smaller.

_____

I would give this student a _____ out of 2, because _____

_____

_____

_____

Lesson 4
MASS AND CAPACITY

Focus Question
What units are used to measure mass and capacity, and how big are those units?

Thinking KAP

Aiden went to the zoo and saw the animals in the picture below.

Which animal is the lightest? _____

Which animal is the heaviest? _____

Touchstones for Capacity

Just as there are many units to measure length, there are many units you can use to measure capacity. Capacity is the measure of how much liquid an object can hold.

Touchstone Table for Capacity

1 cup	about the amount of a drinking glass
1 pint	about the amount of two drinking glasses
1 quart	about the amount of a small container of milk
1 gallon	about the amount of a large container of milk

▌TRY IT OUT▌➡ **Solve the problem below.**

1

3.M.5

Dvora has 1 pint of milk. Which measurement is **smaller** than 1 pint?

A 1 gallon

B 1 pound

C 1 cup

D 1 quart

Explain why you eliminated the wrong answer choices. _____

_____

_____

_____

_____

Reading the Tools

Sometimes a math problem will ask you to read the measurement shown by a diagram. For these problems, all the information you need is in the picture. But you may have to add some information to the diagram before you can find the answer.

❙TRY IT OUT❙➡ **Solve the problem below.**

2 Geoff is measuring milk for a recipe.

How much milk did Geoff measure?

A $\frac{1}{2}$ cup

B 1 cup

C $1\frac{1}{2}$ cups

D 2 cups

Mark the diagram.

What does each small line in the diagram represent? _____

Write in the correct measurements for the unmarked lines.

Touchstones for Weight

You can also use touchstones to help you remember different units for weight. Weight is the measure of how heavy or light an object is.

Touchstone Table for Weight

1 ounce	about the weight of 5 quarters
1 pound	about the weight of 3 apples

Weight can be measured using a scale. There are many different types of scales. There are bathroom scales that you step on, and grocery scales that you put food in.

bathroom scale

grocery scale

▌TRY IT OUT ▌➡ **Find a classroom object that has *approximately* the correct weight.**

1. 2 pounds _____

2. 2 ounces _____

3. 10 pounds _____

4. 10 ounces _____

TRY IT OUT Write your own multiple-choice problem about weight or capacity.

3 _____

_____

_____

_____

A _____

B _____

C _____

D _____

Is your problem about weight or capacity? _____

Would your problem be easy to answer or hard to answer? _____

Why? _____

_____

_____

_____

UNIT 5 (1) (2) (3)

Independent Practice

Use the 4-Step Method for Problem Solving and the strategies you have learned in this lesson to solve the problems in this section.

1 Isabel needs $\frac{3}{4}$ cup of juice. Which cup shows the amount Isabel needs?

3.M.6

A

C

B

D

hint *Mark the measurements on the diagram.*

2 Matt has 1 pint of juice. Which measurement is **bigger** than 1 pint?

3.M.6

A 1 quart

B 1 ounce

C 1 pound

D 1 cup

hint *Eliminate choices that are not units of capacity.*

3

3.M.3

Romeo weighed his suitcase on a scale that measures in pounds. How much does his suitcase weigh?

A 15 pounds

B 18 pounds

C 20 pounds

D 25 pounds

hint ▷ *What does each small line represent?*

4

3.M.6

Mrs. Yasir needs to use 2 cups of sugar. Which choice below shows this amount?

A

C

B

D

hint ▷ *Read each diagram. Which shows 2 cups?*

5 Oliver made 1 quart of lemonade for a party. Which measurement is **smaller** than 1 quart?

3.M.6

    A 1 gallon

    B 1 pound

    C 1 yard

    D 1 cup

hint ▷ *Use your touchstones to help you remember each unit.*

6 Kellie weighed some grapes at the grocery store on a scale that measures in ounces. How many ounces do the grapes weigh?

3.M.3

    A 8 ounces

    B 10 ounces

    C 12 ounces

    D 14 ounces

hint ▷ *What does each line represent?*

7 Which bucket contains the **most** water?

3.M.5

A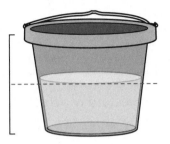

C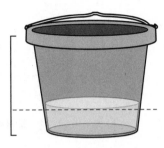

B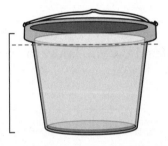

D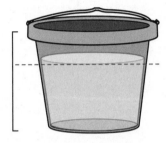

hint ▶ *What is the problem asking you to find?*

8 Zoe wants to measure how much water her bathtub holds. Which measurement will Zoe find?

3.M.4

A the length of the bathtub

B the weight of the bathtub

C the capacity of the bathtub

D the height of the bathtub

hint ▶ *Which choice measures an amount of liquid?*

KAP Wrap

Read the problem and sample student answer below. Then, use the rubric on page 37 to score the student's work.

1

3.M.6

Amir drank 1 quart of water yesterday. What measurement is **smaller** than 1 quart?

Answer   *1 pint*

On the lines below, explain how you know the measurement you wrote is smaller than 1 quart.

It is smaller.

_____

I would give this student a _____ out of 2, because _____

_____

_____

_____

_____

Name_____ Date_____

Mini Practice Test 3

1. Ⓐ Ⓑ Ⓒ Ⓓ   5. Ⓐ Ⓑ Ⓒ Ⓓ   9. Ⓐ Ⓑ Ⓒ Ⓓ

2. Ⓐ Ⓑ Ⓒ Ⓓ   6. Ⓐ Ⓑ Ⓒ Ⓓ   10. Ⓐ Ⓑ Ⓒ Ⓓ

3. Ⓐ Ⓑ Ⓒ Ⓓ   7. Ⓐ Ⓑ Ⓒ Ⓓ   11. Ⓐ Ⓑ Ⓒ Ⓓ

4. Ⓐ Ⓑ Ⓒ Ⓓ   8. Ⓐ Ⓑ Ⓒ Ⓓ   12. Ⓐ Ⓑ Ⓒ Ⓓ

Your answers for questions 13–14 should be written in the test booklet.

1 Helene left for school at 8:10. Which clock shows the time Helene left for school?

A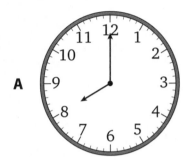

C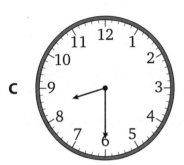

B

D

2 Use your ruler to help you solve this problem.

How many inches long is the eraser shown below?

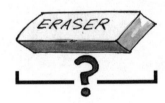

A 1 inch

B $1\frac{1}{2}$ inches

C 2 inches

D $2\frac{1}{2}$ inches

Go On

3 Jullianna cut out a piece of paper to decorate the classroom.

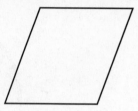

What is the name of the shape that Jullianna cut out?

A rectangle

B square

C hexagon

D rhombus

4 Which shape shows a line of symmetry?

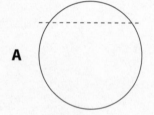

A

C

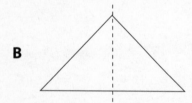

B

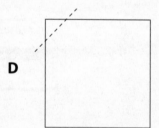

D

5 Which unit of measure is **best** to use for measuring the distance of a four-hour bike ride?

A inch

B foot

C yard

D mile

6 Samir cut two congruent figures out of paper. Which pair of figures did Samir cut out?

A

B

C

D

7 Which unit of measure is **best** to use for measuring the size of a computer mouse?

A   inch

B   foot

C   yard

D   mile

8 Use your ruler to help you solve this problem.

How many inches long is the piece of pasta shown below?

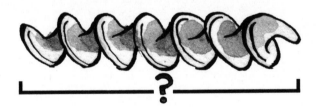

A   2 inches

B $2\frac{1}{2}$ inches

C   3 inches

D   4 inches

Go On

9 What is the shape of the salt shaker shown below?

A cube

B cone

C cylinder

D pyramid

10 Adrianna drew a polygon that had four sides. It had exactly one pair of parallel sides. What shape did Adrianna draw?

A rectangle

B parallelogram

C rhombus

D trapezoid

11 What is the time shown on the clock below?

A 10:05

B 10:25

C 11:05

D 11:25

12 Kendra bought a can of soup shown below.

What shape is the base of the can?

A trapezoid

B triangle

C circle

D square

Go On

13 Alyssa drew the five shapes below.

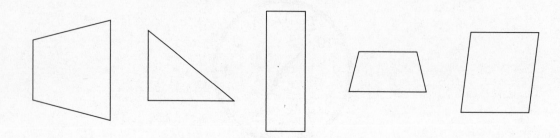

Draw a circle around all of the shapes above that are trapezoids.

On the lines below, describe the properties all trapezoids have in common.

_____

_____

_____

_____

_____

14 Use your ruler to help you solve this problem.

Michele cut a piece of string for an art project. The piece of string is shown below.

How long is Michele's string? Measure to the nearest half-inch.

Answer _____ inches

Michele also needs a second piece of string that is one inch shorter than the one above. How long will the second piece of string be?

Show your work.

Answer _____ inches

Draw the length of the second piece of string in the space below.

STOP

Reflection

Reflect on your work on the Mini Practice Test by completing the table below. First, rate each question by circling either "comfortable" or "challenging." Then, under the "How did you figure out the answer?" column, write the name of the strategy you used to answer each question.

Question	Rate this question!	How did you figure out the answer?
1	Comfortable Challenging	
2	Comfortable Challenging	
3	Comfortable Challenging	
4	Comfortable Challenging	
5	Comfortable Challenging	
6	Comfortable Challenging	
7	Comfortable Challenging	
8	Comfortable Challenging	
9	Comfortable Challenging	
10	Comfortable Challenging	
11	Comfortable Challenging	
12	Comfortable Challenging	

Reflect on Open-Ended Problems

For each problem you got right, describe what really helped you to solve the problem.

- Did you read carefully?
- Did you check your work?
- Did you think back to mistakes you had made before and avoid them?

For each problem you got wrong, describe the error that you made. Based on your answers, give yourself some advice for Test Day.

Question	What did you do to solve the problem that really helped you? or What error did you make?	What advice do you have for yourself on Test Day?
13		
14		

FLPT Full-Length Practice Test

Full-Length Practice Test

1. Ⓐ Ⓑ Ⓒ Ⓓ   15. Ⓐ Ⓑ Ⓒ Ⓓ   29. Ⓐ Ⓑ Ⓒ Ⓓ

2. Ⓐ Ⓑ Ⓒ Ⓓ   16. Ⓐ Ⓑ Ⓒ Ⓓ   30. Ⓐ Ⓑ Ⓒ Ⓓ

3. Ⓐ Ⓑ Ⓒ Ⓓ   17. Ⓐ Ⓑ Ⓒ Ⓓ   31. Ⓐ Ⓑ Ⓒ Ⓓ

4. Ⓐ Ⓑ Ⓒ Ⓓ   18. Ⓐ Ⓑ Ⓒ Ⓓ   32. Ⓐ Ⓑ Ⓒ Ⓓ

5. Ⓐ Ⓑ Ⓒ Ⓓ   19. Ⓐ Ⓑ Ⓒ Ⓓ   33. Ⓐ Ⓑ Ⓒ Ⓓ

6. Ⓐ Ⓑ Ⓒ Ⓓ   20. Ⓐ Ⓑ Ⓒ Ⓓ   34. Ⓐ Ⓑ Ⓒ Ⓓ

7. Ⓐ Ⓑ Ⓒ Ⓓ   21. Ⓐ Ⓑ Ⓒ Ⓓ   35. Ⓐ Ⓑ Ⓒ Ⓓ

8. Ⓐ Ⓑ Ⓒ Ⓓ   22. Ⓐ Ⓑ Ⓒ Ⓓ   36. Ⓐ Ⓑ Ⓒ Ⓓ

9. Ⓐ Ⓑ Ⓒ Ⓓ   23. Ⓐ Ⓑ Ⓒ Ⓓ   37. Ⓐ Ⓑ Ⓒ Ⓓ

10. Ⓐ Ⓑ Ⓒ Ⓓ   24. Ⓐ Ⓑ Ⓒ Ⓓ   38. Ⓐ Ⓑ Ⓒ Ⓓ

11. Ⓐ Ⓑ Ⓒ Ⓓ   25. Ⓐ Ⓑ Ⓒ Ⓓ   39. Ⓐ Ⓑ Ⓒ Ⓓ

12. Ⓐ Ⓑ Ⓒ Ⓓ   26. Ⓐ Ⓑ Ⓒ Ⓓ   40. Ⓐ Ⓑ Ⓒ Ⓓ

13. Ⓐ Ⓑ Ⓒ Ⓓ   27. Ⓐ Ⓑ Ⓒ Ⓓ

14. Ⓐ Ⓑ Ⓒ Ⓓ   28. Ⓐ Ⓑ Ⓒ Ⓓ

Your answers for questions 41–46 should be written in the test booklet.

Mathematics
Book 1

Date: _____

Name: _____

Book 1

TIPS FOR TAKING THE TEST

Here are some suggestions to help you do your best:

- Be sure to read carefully all the directions in the test book.

- Read each question carefully and think about the answer before choosing your response.

 This picture means that you will use your ruler.

1 Eduardo has 6 board games. Roger has 2 board games **fewer** than Eduardo. Which expression can be used to find the number of board games Roger has?

A 6 + 2

B 6 − 2

C 6 × 2

D 6 ÷ 2

2 Which number belongs in the box to make the number sentence correct?

251 < ☐

A 157

B 241

C 251

D 278

3 Ryan has a jar with 693 pennies. What is the value of 9 in the number 693?

A 9

B 90

C 900

D 9,000

4 Laura wants to measure the length of her bookcase. Which tool should Laura use?

A thermometer

B measuring cup

C tape measure

D scale

Go On

5 Janine has the 3 pairs of flip-flop sandals shown below.

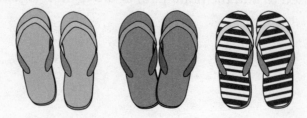

What fraction of Janine's sandals are striped?

A $\frac{1}{4}$

B $\frac{1}{3}$

C $\frac{2}{3}$

D $\frac{3}{1}$

6 Which figures below are congruent?

A

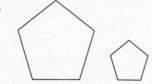

B

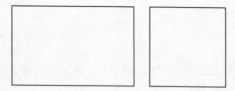

C

D

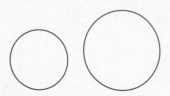

7 Talia has 265 pennies. Evan has 347 pennies. How many **more** pennies does Evan have than Talia?

A 82

B 118

C 367

D 612

8 After buying a bottle of juice, Justin has the bills and coins shown below.

How much money does Justin have left?

A $1.25

B $1.35

C $1.40

D $1.45

Go On

9 Larry writes the number sentence below.

$$\underline{\hspace{2cm}} \times 17 = 17$$

Which number belongs on the line to make the number sentence correct?

A 0

B 1

C 17

D 34

10 Which number belongs in the box to make the number sentence correct?

$$\frac{1}{4} > \square$$

A $\frac{1}{2}$

B $\frac{1}{3}$

C $\frac{1}{4}$

D $\frac{1}{5}$

11 Elijah bought 7 packages of trading cards. Each package has 12 cards. How many trading cards did Elijah buy in all?

A 5

B 19

C 84

D 96

12 The clock below shows the time that Sanjar woke up this morning. What time did Sanjar wake up?

A 7:15

B 7:45

C 8:15

D 8:45

13 Which figure is $\frac{1}{4}$ shaded?

A
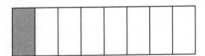

B

C
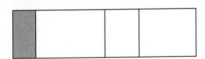

D

Go On

14 Reggie wrote the number sentence below in his math notebook.

$$\underline{\qquad} \times 22 = 0$$

What number belongs on the line to make the number sentence correct?

A 0

B 1

C 11

D 22

15 Which solid figure below has faces that are all squares?

A

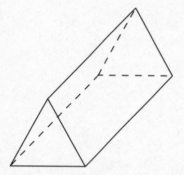

C

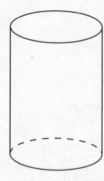

B

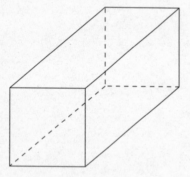

D

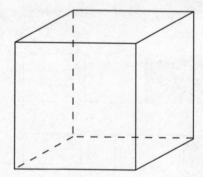

16 The drawing below shows the chairs set up for a piano recital.

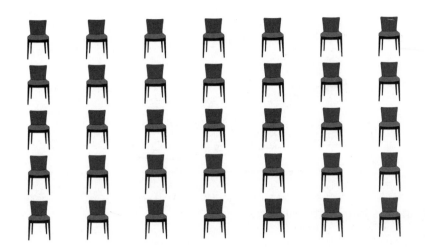

Which expression can be used to find the total number of chairs set up for the recital?

A 5 + 7

B 7 × 5

C 5 + 5 + 5 + 5

D 7 × 7 × 7

17 Mr. Geller has an even number of students in his class. How many students could be in Mr. Geller's class?

A 21

B 23

C 26

D 29

18 Hilliard Elementary School has nine hundred twenty students. What is another way to write nine hundred twenty?

A 92

B 290

C 902

D 920

Go On

19 Use your ruler to help you solve this problem.

Rina cut ribbon for a gift she was wrapping.

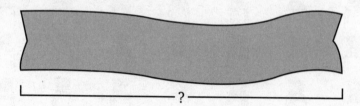

How many inches long is the ribbon?

A $2\frac{1}{2}$

B 3

C $3\frac{1}{2}$

D 4

20 Carla has 48 stickers. She wants to divide them into 8 equal piles. How many stickers should be in each pile?

A 6
B 8
C 12
D 40

21 Keith has 7 marbles. Therese has three times the number of marbles that Keith has. How many marbles does Therese have?

A 3
B 10
C 18
D 21

22 Irina bought two apples for $1.22. Which picture shows $1.22?

A

C

B

D

23 Francesca wants to estimate the sum of the numbers below.

$$22 + 39 + 11$$

Which way is **best** for Francesca to estimate the sum?

A 20 + 30 + 10

B 20 + 30 + 20

C 20 + 40 + 10

D 30 + 40 + 20

Go On

24 Annie drew the pattern below.

♡ ℰ ௧ ℰ ♡ ℰ ௧ ℰ ♡ <u>?</u>

What should be the next figure in Annie's pattern?

A ♡

B ℰ

C ௧

D ℰ

25 The pictograph below shows the number of books four different students read during the month of March.

BOOKS READ IN MARCH

Student	Books Read
Jeremy	📕 📕 📕 📕
Phoebe	📕 📕
Rona	📕 📕 📕
Andy	📕 📕 📕 📕 📕 📕

KEY
📕 = 2 books

Which student read exactly 6 books?

A Jeremy

B Phoebe

C Rona

D Andy

26 $8 \times 6 =$

    A   40

    B   42

    C   48

    D   56

27 Evan is sorting books for the school book fair. There is a box of 196 books, a box of 41 books, and a box of 97 books. What is the **best estimate** of the total number of books in the three boxes?

    A   320

    B   330

    C   340

    D   400

28 There are 7 boxes of rings at a jewelry store. Each box has 4 rings in it. How many rings are there in all?

    A   24

    B   28

    C   32

    D   35

29 There are 63 students in the third grade. They will be separated into equal groups of 9 students each for a field trip. How many groups will there be?

    A   6

    B   7

    C   8

    D   9

Go On

30 There are 14 girls in Mr. Jameson's class. One half of the girls have brown hair. How many girls in Mr. Jameson's class have brown hair?

A 7

B 12

C 16

D 28

31 What number belongs on the line below to make the number sentence true?

$$8 \times \underline{\ ?\ } = 8$$

A 0

B 1

C 16

D 64

32 There are 2,358 students in Woodfield Elementary. There are 1,358 students in Greenfield Elementary. By how much is the number 2,358 greater than 1,358?

A 1 one

B 1 ten

C 1 hundred

D 1 thousand

33 Haley wrote the number sentence below.

$$\square > \frac{1}{3}$$

Which number belongs in the box to make the number sentence true?

A $\frac{1}{2}$

B $\frac{1}{3}$

C $\frac{1}{4}$

D $\frac{1}{5}$

Book 1

34 Nick wrote the number pattern below.

21, 24, 27, __?__, 33

What is the missing number in Nick's number pattern?

A 28
B 29
C 30
D 32

35 Which shape has exactly 5 sides?

A

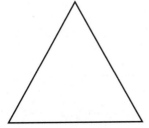

C

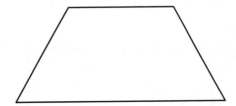

B

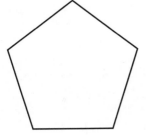

D

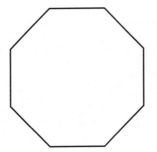

Go On

Book 1

36 Brynn has an ice cream cone like the one shown below.

What is the shape of the top of the ice cream cone?

A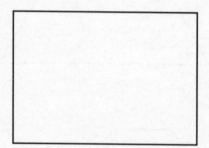

C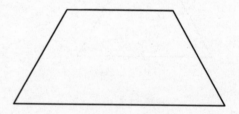

B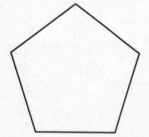

D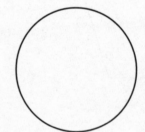

Book 1

37 Dylan spends the coins below to buy a granola bar.

How much money does Dylan spend?

A $0.51

B $0.56

C $0.61

D $0.66

38 Which unit is **best** to measure the length of a pencil?

A inch

B foot

C gram

D yard

Go On

39 The bar graph below shows the number of books Annie bought in the last four months.

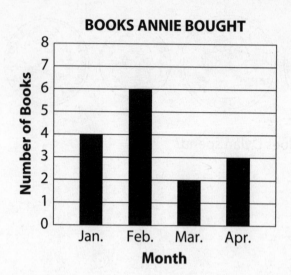

What is the total number of books Annie bought in the four months shown in the graph?

A 6

B 7

C 15

D 16

40 The bar graph below shows the number of miles Victor biked during a four-week period.

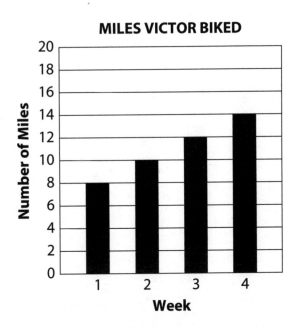

MILES VICTOR BIKED

If the pattern continues for one more week, how many miles will Victor bike in **Week 5**?

A 14

B 16

C 18

D 20

STOP

Mathematics
Book 2

Date: _____

Name: _____

TIPS FOR TAKING THE TEST

Here are some suggestions to help you do your best:

- Be sure to read carefully all the directions in the test book.

- Read each question carefully and think about the answer before writing your response.

- Be sure to show your work when asked. You may receive partial credit if you have shown your work.

 This picture means that you will use your ruler.

41 Lisa wrote the number sentence below.

$$14 \times 9 = 9 \times \underline{\hspace{2cm}}$$

Write a number on the line above to make Lisa's number sentence correct.

Lisa wrote another number sentence below. Write one number on each of the lines below to make the number sentence correct.

$$\underline{\hspace{2cm}} \times 7 = 7 \times \underline{\hspace{2cm}}$$

42 Hillary drew the five shapes below.

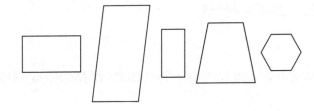

Draw a ring around each shape that is a rectangle.

On the lines below, tell how rectangles are different from other shapes.

_____

_____

_____

_____

Go On

43 Mr. Roya took a survey of his class to find their favorite subject. His results are shown in the tally chart below.

STUDENTS' FAVORITE SUBJECTS

Subject	Number of Students
Math	ЖHT IIII
Science	ЖHT III
History	ЖHT I
English	IIII

What is the total number of students surveyed by Mr. Roya?

Show your work.

Answer _____ students

Complete the bar graph below to show the results of Mr. Roya's study.

Be sure to

- label the blank axis
- graph all the data

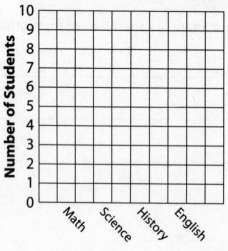

STUDENTS' FAVORITE SUBJECTS

44 Nummy Nibbles ordered new supplies of plates and napkins.

How much did Nummy Nibbles spend on plates and napkins on this order?

Show your work.

Answer $_____

Go On

45 Barry has a collection of special stamps from the post office. Each month, he adds more stamps. The size of his collection is shown in the table below.

BARRY'S STAMP COLLECTION

Month	Number of Stamps in the Collection
January	32
February	35
March	38
April	?

Based on the pattern in the table, how many stamps will Barry have in April?

Answer _____ stamps

On the lines below, describe the rule for the pattern in the table. How did you know how many stamps Barry would have in April?

_____

_____

_____

_____

_____

Book 2

46 There are 6 marbles shown below.

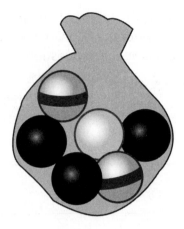

What fraction of the set of marbles are white?

Answer _____

What fraction of the set of marbles are striped?

Answer _____

Draw a ring around $\frac{1}{2}$ of the set of marbles shown below.

STOP

Reflection

Reflect on your work on Book 1 by completing the table below. First, rate each question by circling either "comfortable" or "challenging." Then, under the "How did you figure out the answer?" column, write the name of the strategy you used to answer each question.

Question	Rate this question!	How did you figure out the answer?
1	Comfortable Challenging	
2	Comfortable Challenging	
3	Comfortable Challenging	
4	Comfortable Challenging	
5	Comfortable Challenging	
6	Comfortable Challenging	
7	Comfortable Challenging	
8	Comfortable Challenging	
9	Comfortable Challenging	
10	Comfortable Challenging	
11	Comfortable Challenging	
12	Comfortable Challenging	
13	Comfortable Challenging	
14	Comfortable Challenging	

Question	Rate this question!	How did you figure out the answer?
15	Comfortable Challenging	
16	Comfortable Challenging	
17	Comfortable Challenging	
18	Comfortable Challenging	
19	Comfortable Challenging	
20	Comfortable Challenging	
21	Comfortable Challenging	
22	Comfortable Challenging	
23	Comfortable Challenging	
24	Comfortable Challenging	
25	Comfortable Challenging	
26	Comfortable Challenging	
27	Comfortable Challenging	
28	Comfortable Challenging	
29	Comfortable Challenging	
30	Comfortable Challenging	

Question	Rate this question!	How did you figure out the answer?
31	Comfortable Challenging	
32	Comfortable Challenging	
33	Comfortable Challenging	
34	Comfortable Challenging	
35	Comfortable Challenging	
36	Comfortable Challenging	
37	Comfortable Challenging	
38	Comfortable Challenging	
39	Comfortable Challenging	
40	Comfortable Challenging	

Reflect on Open-Ended Problems

Choose two problems from Book 2 that you answered **correctly**. For each problem, describe what really helped you to solve the problem. For example, did you read carefully? Did you check your work? Did you think back to mistakes you had made before and avoid them? Based on your answer, give yourself some advice for Test Day.

Question	What did you do to solve the problem that really helped you?	What advice do you have for yourself on Test Day?
_____		
_____		

Choose two problems from Book 2 that you answered **incorrectly**. For each problem, describe the error you made. Then, decide what you will do differently on Test Day, and give yourself some advice.

Question	What error did you make?	What advice do you have for yourself on Test Day?
_____		
_____		

APPENDIX A
Extra Practice

3.N.1: Skip-count by 25's, 50's, 100's to 1,000

Fill in the blanks in the patterns below.

1.   125, 150, _____, 200, 225, _____, _____, _____

2.   300, 400, _____, 600, _____, 800, _____, _____

3.   250, 300, 350, _____, _____, _____, _____

4.   150, 250, _____, _____, _____, _____, _____

5.   75, 125, _____, _____, _____, _____, _____

6.   250, 275, _____, _____, _____, 375, _____, _____

7.   80, 105, _____, _____, _____, _____, _____

8.   10, 60, _____, _____, _____, _____, _____

9.   60, 160, _____, _____, 460, _____, _____, _____

10. 385, 410, _____, _____, _____, _____

3.N.2: Read and write whole numbers to 1,000

Write the numbers below in words.

1.   435   _____

2.   628   _____

3.   187   _____

4.   209   _____

5.   98   _____

6.   714   _____

7.   880   _____

8.   120   _____

9.   359   _____

10. 926   _____

3.N.3: Compare and order numbers to 1,000

Write the numbers in order from **least** to **greatest**.

1. 285, 392, 295, 395, 205 _____

2. 875, 870, 880, 890, 980 _____

3. 140, 138, 381, 144, 204 _____

4. 752, 257, 275, 725, 572 _____

5. 43, 304, 403, 443, 430 _____

6. 277, 27, 272, 2, 727 _____

7. 506, 560, 65, 56, 650 _____

Use the symbols $<$, $>$, or = to correctly complete each mathematical statement.

8.   228 ☐ 288   11. 850 ☐ 849

9.   542 ☐ 524   12. 276 ☐ 276

10. 445 ☐ 454   13. 408 ☐ 480

3.N.4: Understand the place value structure of the base ten number system:
   10 ones = 1 ten
   10 tens = 1 hundred
   10 hundreds = 1 thousand

1. In the number 2,950, what digit is in the tens place? _____

2. In the number 2,950, what digit is in the hundreds place? _____

3. In the number 2,950, what digit is in the thousands place? _____

4. In the number 2,950, what digit is in the ones place? _____

5. In which place is the digit 4 in the number 8,724? _____

6. In which place is the digit 7 in the number 8,724? _____

7. In which place is the digit 2 in the number 8,724? _____

8. In which place is the digit 8 in the number 8,724? _____

9. In the number 5,398, what digit is in the thousands place? _____

10. In the number 5,398, what digit is in the ones place? _____

11. In the number 5,398, what digit is in the tens place? _____

KAPLAN ADVANTAGE
NEW YORK MATHEMATICS GRADE 3

© 2010 Kaplan, Inc.

3.N.5: Use a variety of strategies to compose and decompose three-digit numbers

Match each number with its equivalent form.

_____ 1. 54

_____ 2. 88

_____ 3. 725

_____ 4. 395

_____ 5. 401

_____ 6. 927

_____ 7. 833

_____ 8. 116

A. $900 + 20 + 7$

B. $300 + 90 + 5$

C. $10 + 100 + 6$

D. $1 + 1 + 1 + 800 + 30$

E. $5 + 700 + 20$

F. $1 + 1 + 1 + 1 + 50$

G. $400 + 1$

H. $3 + 5 + 80$

Write each number by finding the sum.

9. $300 + 60 + 7 =$ _____

10. $600 + 20 + 4 =$ _____

11. $400 + 80 =$ _____

12. $100 + 6 =$ _____

13. $3 + 10 + 800 =$ _____

14. $1 + 1 + 500 + 70 =$ _____

15. $7 + 10 + 10 + 900 =$ _____

16. $1 + 100 + 100 =$ _____

3.N.6: Use and explain the commutative property of addition and multiplication

1. Which expression results in a product of 32: 8×4 or 4×8?

_____

_____

2. Which equation is more correct: $23 + 18 = 41$ or $18 + 23 = 41$?

_____

Use the commutative property of multiplication to rewrite each problem. Then, find each product.

3. $10 \times 5 =$ _____

4. $2 \times 9 =$ _____

5. $4 \times 5 =$ _____

Use the commutative property of addition to rewrite each problem. Then, find each sum.

6. $11 + 8 =$ _____

7. $22 + 5 =$ _____

8. $53 + 7 =$ _____

3.N.7: Use 1 as the identity element for multiplication

1. Dale says that if he multiplies 1 by 16, the answer is 1. Is Dale correct? Explain your answer.

   _____

   _____

   _____

2. Lyn says that if she multiplies 43 by 1, the answer is 43. Is Lyn correct? Explain your answer.

   _____

   _____

   _____

Find each product.

3. $25 \times 1 =$ _____

4. $1 \times 49 =$ _____

5. $63 \times 1 =$ _____

6. $18 \times 1 =$ _____

7. $1 \times 97 =$ _____

8. $53 \times 1 =$ _____

9. $1 \times 89 =$ _____

10. $72 \times 1 =$ _____

3.N.8: Use the zero property of multiplication

1. Kylie says that if she multiplies 0 and 29, the answer is 0. Is Kylie correct? Explain your answer.

   _____

   _____

   _____

2. Reetu says that if she multiplies 77 and 0, the answer is 1. Is Reetu correct? Explain your answer.

   _____

   _____

   _____

Find each product.

3. $10 \times 0 =$ _____

4. $0 \times 125 =$ _____

5. $38 \times 0 =$ _____

6. $44 \times 0 =$ _____

7. $0 \times 26 =$ _____

8. $17 \times 0 =$ _____

9. $0 \times 9 =$ _____

10. $63 \times 0 =$ _____

3.N.9: Understand and use the associative property of addition

1. Which expression results in a sum of 18: $(8 + 6) + 4$ or $8 + (6 + 4)$?

    _____

    _____

2. Which equation is correct: $(12 + 8) + 6 = 26$ or $12 + (8 + 6) = 26$?

    _____

Use the associative property of addition to rewrite each problem. Then, find each sum.

3. $13 + (7 + 4) =$ _____

4. $13 + (12 + 5) =$ _____

5. $(5 + 7) + 8 =$ _____

6. $(2 + 11) + 9 =$ _____

7. $1 + (19 + 7) =$ _____

3.N.10: Develop an understanding of fractions as part of a whole unit and as parts of a collection

1. Ms. Hillman's class has 28 students. Of those, 3 are named Matthew. What fraction of Ms. Hillman's students are named Matthew? Explain your answer.

    _____

    _____

2. Mindy's cat just had 18 new kittens and 7 of those kittens have striped tails. What fraction of the kittens have a striped tail? Explain your answer.

    _____

    _____

3   Harrison read 14 books over the summer vacation. Of those, 5 were nonfiction. What fraction of the books Harrison read were nonfiction? Explain your answer.

    _____

    _____

3.N.11: Use manipulatives, visual models, and illustrations to name and represent unit fractions $\left(\frac{1}{2}, \frac{1}{3}, \frac{1}{4}, \frac{1}{5}, \frac{1}{6}, \text{and } \frac{1}{10}\right)$ as part of a whole or a set of objects

1. What fraction of the circle below is shaded? Explain your answer.

_____

_____

2. What fraction of the circle below is shaded? Explain your answer.

_____

_____

3. What fraction of the rectangle below is shaded? Explain your answer.

_____

_____

4. How many sections would need to be shaded in the circle below to make it $\frac{1}{5}$ shaded?

_____

_____

5. How many sections would need to be shaded in the rectangle below to make it $\frac{1}{2}$ shaded?

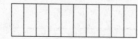

_____

_____

3.N.12: Understand and recognize the meaning of numerator and denominator in the symbolic form of a fraction

1. What is the numerator in the fraction $\frac{3}{7}$? _____

2. What is the denominator in the fraction $\frac{12}{25}$? _____

3. What is the numerator in the fraction $\frac{4}{19}$? _____

4. What is the denominator in the fraction $\frac{3}{13}$? _____

5. Bing says that $\frac{3}{8}$ of her friends are boys. What do the numbers in this fraction mean?

   _____

   _____

6. Nelly says that she ate $\frac{3}{4}$ of an orange. What do the numbers in this fraction mean?

   _____

   _____

7. Gregg wrote a paragraph that took up $\frac{1}{3}$ of a page. What do the numbers in this fraction mean?

   _____

   _____

3.N.13: Recognize fractional numbers as equal parts of a whole

1. Regina has 5 children. Of those children, 2 are girls. What fraction of Regina's children are girls? Explain your answer.

   _____

   _____

2. Lilli bought 8 apples at a farmer's market. Of those apples, 3 are green. What fraction of Lilli's apples are green?

   _____

   _____

3. Karl bumped into a shelf and knocked 4 bottles of water to the floor. The shelf originally had 15 bottles of water on it. What fraction of the water bottles did Karl knock to the floor?

   _____

   _____

© 2010 Kaplan, Inc.

3.N.16: Identify odd and even numbers

Identify each number below as odd or even.

1. 138: _____
2. 213: _____
3. 176: _____
4. 179: _____
5. 15: _____
6. 26: _____
7. 23: _____
8. 802: _____
9. 725: _____
10. 628: _____

11. 555: _____
12. 207: _____
13. 910: _____
14. 332: _____
15. 874: _____
16. 427: _____
17. 13: _____
18. 274: _____
19. 64: _____
20. 717: _____

21. An odd number must have one of five digits in the ones place. What are these numbers?

_____

22. An even number must have one of five digits in the ones place. What are these numbers?

_____

3.N.17: Develop an understanding of the properties of odd/even numbers as a result of addition or subtraction

Find each sum or difference.

1. $5 + 7 =$ _____
2. $3 - 1 =$ _____
3. $9 - 5 =$ _____
4. $3 + 7 =$ _____
5. $1 + 9 =$ _____

6. $2 + 4 =$ _____
7. $6 - 2 =$ _____
8. $8 + 10 =$ _____
9. $4 + 8 =$ _____
10. $10 - 6 =$ _____

11. $1 + 10 =$ _____
12. $8 - 3 =$ _____
13. $3 + 6 =$ _____
14. $8 + 7 =$ _____
15. $9 - 2 =$ _____

Based on your work above, answer the following questions.

16. Look at problems #1–5. Then complete the statement:

odd + odd = _____   odd − odd = _____

17. Look at problems #6–10. Then complete the statement:

even + even = _____   even − even = _____

18. Look at problems #11–15. Then complete the statements:

even + odd = _____   even − odd = _____

odd + even = _____   odd − even = _____

3.N.18: Use a variety of strategies to add and subtract 3-digit numbers (with and without regrouping)

Find each sum or difference.

1. 324 + 511 = _____

2. 172 + 316 = _____

3. 243 + 392 = _____

4. 803 − 415 = _____

5. 678 + 827 = _____

6. 596 − 144 = _____

7. 227 + 318 = _____

8. 873 − 798 = _____

9. Belinda had 185 marbles in her collection. Randy had 156 marbles in his collection.
   - How many marbles do they have all together? _____
   - How many **more** marbles does Belinda have than Randy? _____

10. Carly counted 276 books on one shelf in the library. She counted 316 books on another shelf. How many books did Carly count on the two bookshelves all together?

   _____

11. Jorge read 343 pages in June. He read 235 pages in July. How many **more** pages did Jorge read in June than July?

   _____

3.N.19: Develop fluency with single-digit multiplication facts

Find each product.

1. 12 × 5 = _____

2. 11 × 6 = _____

3. 4 × 13 = _____

4. 8 × 10 = _____

5. 5 × 13 = _____

6. 15 × 3 = _____

7. 70 × 9 = _____

8. 18 × 5 = _____

9. 6 × 12 = _____

10. 7 × 12 = _____

11. 11 × 8 = _____

12. 4 × 15 = _____

13. 7 × 10 = _____

14. 9 × 12 = _____

15. 6 × 11 = _____

16. If flowers cost $3 each, what is the cost for 5 flowers? _____

17. A box of paper clips costs $4. What is the cost for 6 boxes? _____

18. A booklet has 8 pages inside. What is the total number of pages in 5 booklets? _____

19. Erika puts 3 ice cubes in every glass of water. If she pours 7 glasses of water, how many ice cubes does Erika need? _____

20. Juice boxes come in packs of 4. If Ms. Lyman buys 3 packs, how many juice boxes does she buy?

   _____

3.N.20: Use a variety of strategies to solve multiplication problems with factors up to 12 × 12

Multiply.

1. $6 \times 2 \times 4 = $ _____
2. $3 \times 5 \times 10 = $ _____
3. $9 \times 2 \times 8 = $ _____
4. $11 \times 1 \times 7 = $ _____
5. $5 \times 3 \times 12 = $ _____
6. $6 \times 9 \times 5 = $ _____
7. $8 \times 3 \times 10 = $ _____
8. $2 \times 9 \times 5 = $ _____
9. $4 \times 12 \times 3 = $ _____
10. $12 \times 1 \times 9 = $ _____

11. $7 \times 2 \times 1 \times 3 = $ _____
12. $10 \times 2 \times 8 \times 5 = $ _____
13. $6 \times 12 \times 5 \times 2 = $ _____
14. $8 \times 2 \times 2 \times 2 = $ _____
15. $3 \times 3 \times 10 \times 3 = $ _____
16. $3 \times 2 \times 4 \times 6 = $ _____
17. $1 \times 11 \times 4 \times 3 = $ _____
18. $6 \times 1 \times 7 \times 1 = $ _____
19. $10 \times 2 \times 4 \times 5 = $ _____
20. $2 \times 3 \times 3 \times 5 = $ _____

21. What properties of multiplication did you use to solve the problems above?

   _____

   _____

3.N.21: Use the area model, tables, patterns, arrays, and doubling to provide meaning for multiplication

Look at the array of balloons below.

1. How many rows of balloons are there? _____

2. How many columns of balloons are there? _____

3. What multiplication expression can be used to determine how many balloons there are?

   _____

4. Use the expression to find the total number of balloons.

   _____

3.N.22: Demonstrate fluency and apply single-digit division facts

Find each quotient.

1. $24 \div 3 =$ _____

2. $52 \div 13 =$ _____

3. $15 \div 5 =$ _____

4. $72 \div 9 =$ _____

5. $32 \div 4 =$ _____

6. $65 \div 13 =$ _____

7. $20 \div 5 =$ _____

8. $48 \div 16 =$ _____

9. $50 \div 10 =$ _____

10. $60 \div 10 =$ _____

11. $14 \div 2 =$ _____

12. $80 \div 10 =$ _____

13. $18 \div 6 =$ _____

14. $55 \div 11 =$ _____

15. $10 \div 5 =$ _____

16. $77 \div 11 =$ _____

17. $6 \div 2 =$ _____

18. $81 \div 9 =$ _____

19. $27 \div 9 =$ _____

20. $56 \div 7 =$ _____

21. $9 \div 3 =$ _____

22. $84 \div 12 =$ _____

23. $36 \div 4 =$ _____

24. $24 \div 12 =$ _____

25. Donny has 18 stickers to divide between 6 friends. How many stickers should each friend get?

_____

26. Liza is planting 27 tomato plants in 3 rows. How many plants should be in each row?

_____

27. Laneesha has 5 days to do an art project. It will take her 15 hours to complete the project. She works on the project for the same amount of time each day. How many hours a day does Laneesha spend on the art project?

_____

28. $24 is divided equally among 4 friends. How much does each friend receive?

_____

29. If there are 36 sheets of paper to be given to twelve groups, how many sheets of paper will each group receive?

_____

30. $99 is to be divided evenly among your eleven friends. How much money should each person expect to receive?

_____

Find a pattern between the numbers in the top row and the numbers in the bottom row. Then, complete each table.

1.

36	28	12	24		8		16	
9	7	3	6	1		5		8

2.

12	36		6		54	18	42	24
2		8	1	5	9		7	4

3. Use the blocks below to make three identical groups.

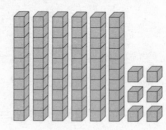

How many blocks are in each group? _____

_____

4. Show how $51.25 can be divided among 5 friends.

How much money does each person receive? _____

3.N.24: Develop strategies for selecting the appropriate computational and operational method in problem solving situations

1. Sixteen friends are going on a rafting trip. Four people can ride in each boat. Explain how you would find how many boats are needed.

    _____

2. Henrietta and Bryan went apple picking. Henrietta picked 14 apples and Bryan picked 9 apples. Explain how you would find how many **more** apples Henrietta picked than Bryan.

    _____

3. There were 289 people at the school play on Friday. There were 317 people at the school play on Saturday. Explain how you would find the total number of people at the school play on Friday and Saturday.

    _____

4. Jossia has 5 bookshelves in her room. She keeps 9 books on each shelf. Explain how you would find the total number of books in Jossia's room.

    _____

5. Last year, there were 514 students in the third grade. This year, there are 329 students in the third grade. Explain how you would find how many **more** students were in third grade last year than this year.

    _____

6. Nikki collected 118 shells at the beach over the summer. Laila collected 223 shells at the beach over the summer. Explain how many shells Nikki and Laila collected all together.

    _____

7. Kenneth bought 3 packages of trading cards. Each package contains 7 cards. Explain how to find out how many trading cards Kenneth bought in all.

    _____

8. Nisha printed out 32 flyers and put them into 4 equal piles. Explain how to find how many flyers are in each pile.

    _____

3.N.25: Estimate numbers up to 200

Round to the nearest ten.

1. 79 _____
2. 412 _____
3. 35 _____
4. 356 _____
5. 69 _____

6. 384 _____
7. 107 _____
8. 393 _____
9. 82 _____
10. 428 _____

11. 150 _____
12. 331 _____
13. 77 _____
14. 489 _____
15. 134 _____

Round to the nearest hundred.

1. 236 _____
2. 21 _____
3. 467 _____
4. 123 _____
5. 277 _____

6. 42 _____
7. 222 _____
8. 173 _____
9. 241 _____
10. 199 _____

11. 454 _____
12. 52 _____
13. 258 _____
14. 163 _____
15. 309 _____

3.N.26: Recognize real world situations in which an estimate (rounding) is more appropriate

1. A pen costs $4.15. Estimate the cost of 5 such pens. _____

2. The weekly wage of a worker is $365. Round the amount to the nearest hundred. _____

3. Matt and Justin went to a theme park. They spent $214. Round the amount they spent to the nearest hundred. _____

4. 2,216 people visited an arts exhibition during a weekend. Round the number of visitors to the nearest hundred. _____

5. A company sold 6,233 refrigerators in a year. Round the number of refrigerators sold to the nearest ten. _____

6. Paul wanted to donate money to orphans. To raise money, he conducted an orchestra for 3 days. On the first day, he collected $426, on the second day $289, and on the third day $178. Estimate the amount of money collected in 3 days to the nearest hundred. _____

3.N.27: Check reasonableness of an answer by using estimation

1. Estimate the quotient of 100 ÷ 5. _____

2. Elian counted the number of girls and boys in his school. There are 315 boys and 383 girls.
   Estimate the total number of students to the nearest hundred. _____

3. Rick had 67 trading cards. He gave 23 to his friend. About how many cards did he have
   left? _____

4. Mindi rides her bike 11 miles every day. About how many miles will she ride in 9 days? _____
   _____

5. It takes Helene about 53 minutes to make a bracelet. About how many bracelets could she
   make in 3 hours? _____

6. Kwan-Yi has $42. She wants to buy some T-shirts that cost $9 each. About how many T-shirts
   can she buy? _____

7. At a batting cage, Chris hit 58 baseballs. Tanya hit 72 baseballs. About how many **more** did
   Tanya hit than Chris? _____

3.A.1: Use the symbols $<$, $>$, $=$ (with and without the use of a number line) to compare whole numbers and unit fractions $\left(\dfrac{1}{2}, \dfrac{1}{3}, \dfrac{1}{4}, \dfrac{1}{5}, \dfrac{1}{6}, \text{and } \dfrac{1}{10}\right)$

Use the number line below to fill in the blanks with the correct symbol: $<$, $>$, or $=$.

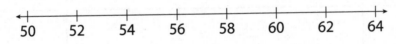

1. 56 ☐ 50

2. 66 ☐ 60

3. 54 ☐ 64

4. 50 ☐ 50

5. 56 ☐ 66

6. 58 ☐ 54

Compare the numbers and use the symbols $<$, $>$, or $=$ to make a true sentence.

7. $\dfrac{2}{3}$ ☐ $\dfrac{1}{4}$

8. $\dfrac{1}{5}$ ☐ $\dfrac{3}{10}$

9. $\dfrac{4}{6}$ ☐ $\dfrac{2}{3}$

10. $\dfrac{1}{2}$ ☐ $\dfrac{7}{10}$

11. $\dfrac{3}{5}$ ☐ $\dfrac{1}{3}$

12. $\dfrac{2}{4}$ ☐ $\dfrac{3}{6}$

3.A.2: Describe and extend numeric (+, −) and geometric patterns

Write a rule to describe each number pattern. Then, write the next four terms.

1. 6, 11, 16, 21,…   _____   _____, _____, _____, _____

2. 86, 80, 74, 68,…   _____   _____, _____, _____, _____

3. 9, 12, 15, 18,…   _____   _____, _____, _____, _____

4. 2, 14, 26, 38,…   _____   _____, _____, _____, _____

5. 34, 32, 30, 28,…   _____   _____, _____, _____, _____

6. 65, 58, 51, 44,…   _____   _____, _____, _____, _____

7.

How many circles will be in the next term of the sequence? _____

3.G.1: Define and use correct terminology when referring to shapes (circle, triangle, square, rectangle, rhombus, trapezoid, and hexagon)

Complete the table.

		Number of Sides	Number of Equal Sides	Pairs of Parallel Sides	Name of Shape
1.					
2.					
3.					
4.					
5.					
6.					
7.					
8.					

3.G.2: Identify congruent and similar figures

Are the figures congruent or similar?

1.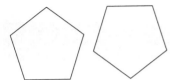

_____

2.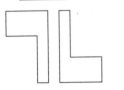

_____

3.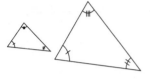

_____

4.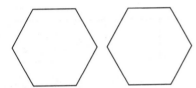

_____

5.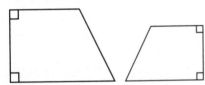

_____

6.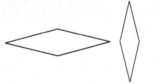

_____

7.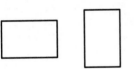

_____

8.

_____

9.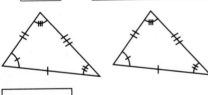

_____

10.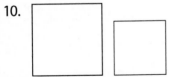

_____

3.G.3: Name, describe, compare, and sort three-dimensional shapes: cube, cylinder, sphere, prism, and cone

Complete the table.

		Number of Faces	Shape and Number of Bases	Name of Shape
1.				
2.				
3.				
4.				
5.				
6.				

7. Which shape **best** describes the globe below?

_____

8. Which shape **best** describes the shoe box below?

_____

9. Which shape **best** describes the salt shaker below?

_____

3.G.4: Identify the faces on a three-dimensional shape as two-dimensional shapes

Answer the questions about each three-dimensional figure.

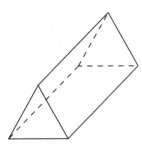

1. What is the name of this figure? _____
2. How many bases does this figure have? _____
3. What are the shapes of the bases? _____
4. How many other faces does this figure have? _____
5. What are the shapes of these faces? _____

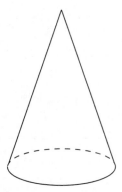

6. What is the name of this figure? _____
7. How many bases does this figure have? _____
8. What shape is the base? _____

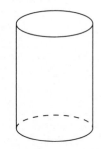

9. What is the name of this figure? _____
10. How many bases does this figure have? _____
11. What shape are the bases? _____

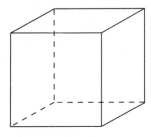

12. What is the name of this figure? _____
13. How many total faces does this figure have? _____
14. What shape are the faces? _____

3.G.5: Identify and construct lines of symmetry

1. How many lines of symmetry does the figure below have?

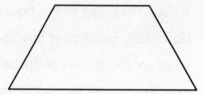

2. How many lines of symmetry does the figure below have?

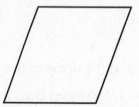

3. Draw all of the lines of symmetry on the figure below.

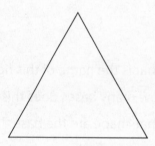

4. Draw all of the lines of symmetry on the figure below.

3.M.1: Select tools and units (customary) appropriate for the length measured

1. Which tool would be **best** to measure the height of a door—a tape measure, a scale, or a measuring cup? Explain your answer.

   _____

   _____

2. Which is the **best** unit to measure the length of a pencil—inch, foot, or yard? Explain your answer.

   _____

   _____

3. Which tool would be **best** to measure the length of an eraser—a ruler, a thermometer, or a scale?

   _____

   _____

4. Which is the **most likely** measurement for the height of a chair—3 inches, 3 feet, or 3 yards?

   _____

   _____

5. What is the **most likely** measurement for the distance between houses in two different towns—15 inches, 15 feet, or 15 miles?

   _____

   _____

6. What is the **most likely** measurement for the length of a car—10 inches, 10 feet, or 10 miles?

   _____

   _____

7. Which unit would be **best** to measure the length of a jump rope—inch, foot, or mile?

   _____

   _____

8. Which tool would be **best** to measure the length of a dollar bill—a ruler, a measuring spoon, or a clock?

   _____

   _____

3.M.2: Use a ruler/yardstick to measure to the nearest standard unit (whole and $\frac{1}{2}$ inches, whole feet, and whole yards)

Use a ruler to measure each object and fill in the blanks.

1. ⊢—————————————————⊣

The crayon is _____ inches long.

2. ⊢

The height of the flower is _____ inches.

3. ⊢—————————————————⊣

How long is the arrow? _____ inches

4.

How tall is the star? _____ inches

© 2010 Kaplan, Inc.

3.M.3: Measure objects, using ounces and pounds

1. Is the mass of a textbook **most likely** 2 ounces or 2 pounds? _____

2. Which is **more likely** the weight of a party hat—4 ounces or 4 pounds?

_____

3. Callie wants to measure the weight of her puppy in pounds and ounces. Which of the three objects below should Callie use?

_____

3.M.4: Recognize capacity as an attribute that can be measured

1. Which measurement would be the **best** way to find out how much water a bathtub holds—mass, height, or capacity?

_____

_____

2. Which of the three figures below could be measured for capacity?

_____

_____

3. Which tool would be **best** to measure the capacity of a drinking glass?

_____

3.M.5: Compare capacities (e.g., Which contains more? Which contains less?)

1. Which of the boxes below has a **greater** capacity?

2. Which of the cones below has a **lesser** capacity—the party hat or the traffic cone?

3.M.6: Measure capacity, using cups, pints, quarts, and gallons

1. Is the capacity of a coffee mug **most likely** 1 cup or 1 quart? _____

2. Which is **more likely** the capacity of a bathtub—50 ounces, 50 pints, or 50 gallons?

3. Kyle wants to measure the capacity of a water bottle. Which of the three objects below should Kyle use?

3.M.7: Count and represent combined coins and dollars, using currency symbols ($0.00)

1. Henrik spent the money below on new pencils.

How much did Henrik spend? _____

2. Jessica donated the amount below to a charity.

How much did Jessica donate? _____

3. Adrian emptied his piggy bank and found the following coins.

How much money was in Adrian's piggy bank? _____

4. Tinh added the coins below to a tip jar.

How much money did Tinh put in the tip jar? _____

APPENDICES

3.M.8: Relate unit fractions to the face of the clock: Whole = 60 minutes, $\frac{1}{2}$ = 30 minutes, $\frac{1}{4}$ = 15 minutes

1. How many minutes are in one quarter $\left(\frac{1}{4}\right)$ of an hour?

2. If something takes a half hour, how many minutes is that?

3. Vella started a project at 4:45 P.M.

She spent $\frac{1}{4}$ hour working on the project. What time did Vella finish? _____

4. If the minute hand travels completely around the face of a clock, how many minutes have passed?

_____

5. Hinna starts running at 11:00 A.M.

If she runs for $\frac{1}{2}$ hour, at what time does Hinna stop running? _____

KAPLAN ADVANTAGE
NEW YORK MATHEMATICS GRADE 3

3.M.9: Tell time to the minute, using digital and analog clocks

1. Rina threw a party at the time shown on the clock below.

What time did Rina's party start? _____

2. Alana leaves for school at the time shown on the clock below.

What time does Alana leave for school? _____

3. Dexter has a digital clock on his desk.

Write the time shown on the clock in words. _____

4. Nolan got home from swim practice at the time shown on the clock below.

What time did Nolan get home from practice? _____

3.M.10: Select and use standard (customary) and non-standard units to estimate measurements

1. Which of the following is **most likely** the weight of a puppy—8 ounces, 8 pounds, or 8 tons?

    _____

2. Which of the following is **most likely** the height of a door—8 inches, 8 feet, or 8 yards?

    _____

3. Which of the following is **most likely** the capacity of a drinking glass—2 ounces, 2 cups, or 2 quarts?

    _____

4. Which of the following is **most likely** the weight of a piece of paper—1 ounce, 1 pound, or 1 ton?

    _____

5. Which of the following is **most likely** the length of a pencil—6 inches, 6 feet, or 6 yards?

    _____

6. Look at the arrow below.

    About how many paper clips long is the arrow?

    _____

7. Which of the following is **most likely** the capacity of a kitchen sink—4 cups, 4 pints, or 4 gallons?

    _____

8. Look at the rectangle below.

    About how many circles long is the rectangle?

    _____

3.S.3: Construct a frequency table to represent a collection of data

1. Tia surveyed some of her friends to find out their favorite fruits. Her results are shown below.

bananas	apples	bananas	oranges
oranges	apples	oranges	oranges
strawberries	bananas	strawberries	oranges
bananas	oranges	strawberries	apples
oranges	apples	bananas	bananas

Use the information above to complete the frequency table below.

Type of Fruit	Frequency
Bananas	
Apples	
Oranges	
Strawberries	

2. Lincoln surveyed some of his friends to find out their favorite ride at the amusement park. His results are shown below.

bumper cars	water slide	bumper cars	bumper cars
roller coaster	roller coaster	tilt-a-whirl	roller coaster
roller coaster	bumper cars	Ferris wheel	tilt-a-whirl
tilt-a-whirl	roller coaster	Ferris wheel	roller coaster
bumper cars	tilt-a-whirl	roller coaster	Ferris wheel

Use the information above to complete the frequency table below.

Favorite Ride	Frequency
Bumper Cars	
Roller Coaster	
Tilt-A-Whirl	
Ferris Wheel	
Water Slide	

3.S.4: Identify the parts of pictographs and bar graphs

Use the pictograph below to answer questions 1 and 2.

FLOWERS IN GARDENS

Name	Number of Flowers
Julie	🌸 🌸 🌸 🌸 🌸
Reetu	🌸 🌸
Jamal	🌸 🌸 🌸
Jung	🌸 🌸 🌸 🌸

KEY
🌸 = 2 flowers

1. What is the title of the graph? _____

2. The key says that each picture of a flower is equal to _____.

Use the bar graph below to answer questions 3–5.

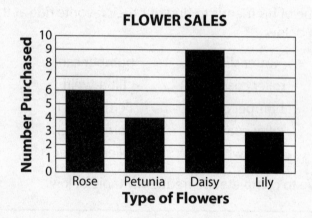

3. What is the title of the graph? _____

4. What do the numbers on the vertical axis show? _____

5. What is the difference between the different bars? _____

_____

3.S.5: Display data in pictographs and bar graphs

1. Farheed interviewed 20 of his classmates to find out their favorite vegetable. He displayed his data in the table below. Use the data to complete the bar graph.

FAVORITE VEGETABLES

Type of Vegetable	Number of Votes
Broccoli	6
Spinach	4
Carrots	8
Asparagus	2

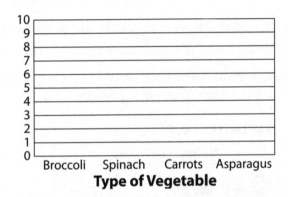

2. Use the same information from the table above to complete the pictograph below.

FAVORITE VEGETABLES

Types of Vegetable	Number of Votes

KEY
= 2 votes

3.S.6: State the relationship between pictographs and bar graphs

Four students participated in a Walk-A-Thon at their school. The graph below shows how many laps they each walked. Use the bar graph to answer questions 1 and 2.

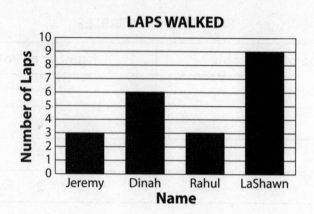

1. If you were to put this data into a pictograph, what would the left column title be? _____

2. If the key in the new pictograph shows that each icon equals 3 laps, how many icons would you draw for Dinah? _____

Bijal asked some of her classmates to name their favorite subject at school. The results are shown in the pictograph below. Use the graph to answer questions 3–5.

FAVORITE SUBJECT

Subject	Number of Votes
Math	●●●
English	●●●●●
Social Studies	●●●●●●
Science	●●●●

KEY
● = 1 vote

3. If you converted this data into a bar graph, what would the vertical label be?

_____

4. What would the title of the bar graph be? _____

5. How tall would the bar for English be? _____

3.S.7: Read and interpret data in bar graphs and pictographs

Use the graph below to answer questions 1–3.

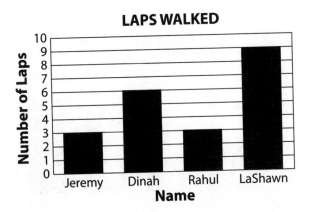

1. How many laps did Jeremy walk? _____

2. How many **more** laps did LaShawn walk than Rahul? _____

3. How many laps did the four friends walk all together? _____

Use the graph below to answer questions 4–6.

FAVORITE SUBJECT

Subject	Number of Votes
Math	● ● ●
English	● ● ● ● ●
Social Studies	● ● ● ● ● ●
Science	● ● ● ●

KEY
● = 1 vote

4. How many students picked social studies as their favorite subject? _____

5. How many students picked math as their favorite subject? _____

6. How many students picked either English or science as their favorite subject? _____

3.S.8: Formulate conclusions and make predictions from graphs

Ella counted the number of fruits on her apple tree over 4 weeks. The data she collected is displayed in the bar graph below. Use the graph below to answer questions 1–3.

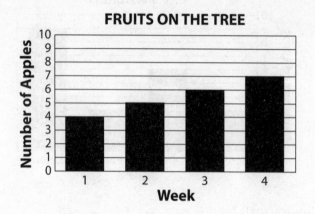

FRUITS ON THE TREE

1. What is the pattern shown in the graph? _____

2. How many apples would you predict to be on the tree in Week 5? _____

3. How many apples would you predict to be on the tree in Week 8? _____

Mr. Gonzalez led a canned food drive in his classroom. He counted how many cans he collected every week and kept track of the data in a pictograph. Use the pictograph below to answer questions 4–6.

CANS COLLECTED

Week	Number of Cans
1	🥫 🥫
2	🥫 🥫 🥫
3	🥫 🥫 🥫 🥫
4	🥫 🥫 🥫 🥫 🥫

KEY

🥫 = 5 cans

4. What is the pattern shown in the graph? _____

5. How many cans in all would you predict will be collected in Week 5? _____

6. How many cans in all would you predict will be collected in Week 7 _____

APPENDIX B
Glossary

Number Names

Whole Numbers

Number	English Name	Nombre en Español
1	one	uno
2	two	dos
3	three	tres
4	four	cuatro
5	five	cinco
6	six	seis
7	seven	siete
8	eight	ocho
9	nine	nueve
10	ten	diez
11	eleven	once
12	twelve	doce
13	thirteen	trece
14	fourteen	catorce
15	fifteen	quince
16	sixteen	diez y seis
17	seventeen	diez y siete
18	eighteen	diez y ocho
19	nineteen	diez y nueve
20	twenty	veinte

Number	English Name	Nombre en Español
21	twenty-one	veinte y uno
22	twenty-two	veinte y dos
23	twenty-three	veinte y tres
24	twenty-four	veinte y cuatro
25	twenty-five	veinte y cinco
26	twenty-six	veinte y seis
27	twenty-seven	veinte y siete
28	twenty-eight	veinte y ocho
29	twenty-nine	veinte y nueve
30	thirty	treinta
40	forty	cuaranta
50	fifty	cinquenta
60	sixty	sesenta
70	seventy	setenta
80	eighty	ochenta
90	ninety	noventa
100	one hundred	cién
1,000	one thousand	mil
100,000	one hundred thousand	cien miles
1,000,000	one million	millón

Fractions

Number	Diagram	English Name	Nombre en Español
$\frac{1}{2}$		one-half	mitad
$\frac{1}{3}$		one-third	tercer
$\frac{1}{4}$		one-fourth	cuarto
$\frac{1}{5}$		one-fifth	quinto
$\frac{1}{6}$		one-sixth	sexto
$\frac{1}{8}$		one-eighth	octavo
$\frac{1}{10}$		one-tenth	décimo

APPENDICES

Glossary

A

acute angle (*el ángulo agudo*) An angle which measures between 0° and 90°.

acute triangle (*el triángulo agudo*) A triangle with three acute angles. An acute angle measures between 0° and 90°.

algebra (*el algebra*) The area of mathematics that involves writing math statements in a general way. In algebra, unknown numbers are called *variables* and are represented by letters. For example, 4 less than a number, *x*, is written as $x - 4$.

algebraic expression (*una expresión algebraica*) A quantity written using numbers and variables. This may or may not contain operations, but will not contain a relation symbol. For example, x, $x + 7$, and $3x$ are algebraic expressions.

algebraic patterns (*unas configuraciones alegbraicas*) An arrangement of numbers that follow a rule. For example, the two groups of numbers below follow the algebraic pattern "multiply by 2." The numbers in Column 2 are twice the numbers in Column 1.

Column 1	Column 2
2	4
3	6
4	8
5	10
6	12

The pattern is "multiply by 2."

algebraic relationship (*una relación algebraica*) Two sets of numbers have an algebraic relationship if the numbers follow a rule such as "add 1," "multiply by 3," or "divide by 2." For example, the two groups of numbers below have an algebraic relationship because they follow the rule "divide by 2." Each number in Column 2 is half of the number in Column 1.

Column 1	Column 2
2	1
4	2
6	3
8	4
10	5

The relationship is "divide by 2."

algebraically (*algebraico*): In terms of variables (letters) and numbers.

analog clock (*un reloj análogo*): A timepiece (clock) that has hour and minute hands.

angle (*el ángulo*) A figure formed by two lines with a common endpoint. The common endpoint is called the *vertex* of the angle.

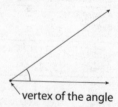

vertex of the angle

ante meridian, A.M. (*antes del medio día*) The label given to the hours between 12:00 midnight and 12:00 noon. It describes the morning hours. For example, 8:00 A.M. is 8 o'clock in the morning.

area (*el area*) The number of square units needed to cover a flat region. For example, the area of the rectangle shown is 8 square feet.

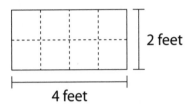

2 feet

4 feet

Area = 8 square feet

arithmetic expression (*una expresión aritmética*) A combination of numbers with one or more arithmetic operations. For example, $3 + 2$, and $(8 - 3) \div 5$.

array (*una serie, una colección, un grupo*) A rectangular arrangement of objects in equal rows or columns.

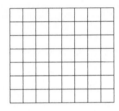

associative property (*la propiedad asociativa*) The order in which you group numbers does not change the sum or product. For example, $(2 + 4) + 6 = 2 + (4 + 6)$ and $(2 \times 4) \times 6 = 2 \times (4 \times 6)$.

attribute (*un atributo*) A property or quality of a number or object. For example, three attributes of the number 16 are that it is even, a multiple of 8, and a square number.

axis (*el eje*) The vertical and horizontal lines that divide the coordinate plane into quadrants. The horizontal axis is the x-axis, and the vertical axis is the y-axis. The plural is "axes" (*los ejes*).

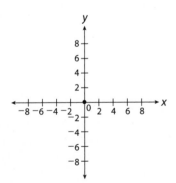

B

bar graph (*una gráfica de barra*) A graph that uses vertical or horizontal bars to indicate relationships among data.

base-ten number system (*el sistema de numeración de la base diez*) The number system that uses place values such as ones, tens, hundreds, thousands, etc., to the left of the decimal point. It uses tenths, hundredths, thousandths, etc., to the right of the decimal point.

C

calculate (*calcular*) To add, subtract, multiply, and divide numbers.

calendar (*el calendario*) A chart used to keep track of dates. One year has 12 months. With the exception of February, each month has 30 or 31 days.

capacity (*la capacidad*) The amount of space in a container such as a box or a bottle. For example, if a bottle contains 12 ounces of water, then the capacity of the bottle is 12 ounces.

centimeter (*un centímetro*) A unit of length in the metric system, abbreviated as "cm". There are 100 centimeters in 1 meter.

circle (*un círculo*) The set of all points on a flat surface that are at the same distance from the center, a point on that surface.

classify triangles (*clasificar triángulos*) To group triangles by their attributes. For example, a triangle is isosceles if only two of its sides and angles are equal.

closed figure (*una figura cerada*) A flat figure or shape in which the beginning and end points touch. There are no line breaks or missing sides on a closed figure. Circles, squares, and rectangles are examples of closed figures.

coin (*una moneda*) Pennies, nickels, dimes, and quarters are examples of coins.

APPENDICES

common denominators (*los denominadores communes*) Two or more denominators that are the same. For example, $\frac{4}{9}$ and $\frac{8}{9}$ share a common denominator, which is 9. Also called "like denominators."

common factor (*el factor común*) A number which divides evenly into two or more numbers. For example, 7 is a common factor of 21 and 35 because $21 \div 7 = 3$ and $35 \div 7 = 5$.

common multiple (*el múltiplo común*) A number which is a multiple of 2 or more numbers. For example, 24 is a common multiple of 8 and 12 because $8 \times 3 = 24$ and $12 \times 2 = 24$.

commutative property of addition (*la propiedad comutativa de adición*) The order in which numbers are added does not change their sum. For example, $3 + 5 = 5 + 3$.

commutative property of multiplication (*la propiedad comutativa de la multiplicación*) The order in which numbers are multiplied does not change their product. For example, $3 \times 5 = 5 \times 3$.

compare a number (*comparer un númera*) To judge the size of a number or object as it relates to the size of another number or object.

compatible numbers (*los números compatibles*) Pairs of numbers that are easy to compute mentally. For example, when adding $7 + 22 + 3$, add compatible numbers $7 + 3$ first because the sum is easy to compute.

compose a number (*componer un número*) To form a number using other numbers. For example, 10 can be composed of 5 and 5, 6 and 4, 7 and 3, etc.

composite number (*un número compuesto*) An integer greater than 1 with more than two factors. For example, 10 is a composite number because its factors are 1, 2, 5, and 10.

conclusion (*una conclusión*) A statement which represents the result or outcome of a problem or experiment.

cone (*un cono*) A solid with a circular base whose surface converges to a point not on the base.

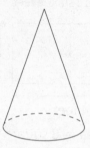

congruent (*congruente*) Having the same shape and the same size. The two squares shown below are congruent.

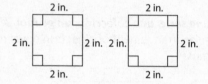

The two triangles shown below are congruent.

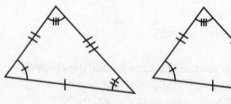

constant (*un constante*) A number or symbol representing a value that does not change. For example, 5 is a constant because its value always stays the same.

convert (*converter*) To express a given measurement in terms of a different unit of measurement. For example, 2 yards can be converted to feet using the fact that 1 yard equals 3 feet. Therefore, 2 yards equals 6 feet.

coordinate plane (*el sistema de coordenadas plano*) A plane formed by a horizontal line (*x*-axis) and a vertical line (*y*-axis). The plane is divided into four quadrants in which ordered pairs, or points, are plotted.

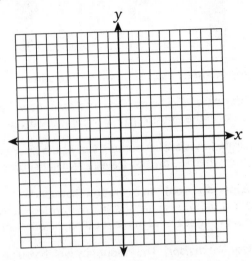

corresponding angles (*unos ángulos correspondientes*) Angles that are in the same position in two or more similar polygons are corresponding and equal. For example, ∠A and ∠B are corresponding angles.

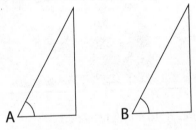

corresponding sides (*unos lados correspondientes*) In similar polygons, sides in the same position are corresponding and proportional. For example, AB and DE are corresponding sides.

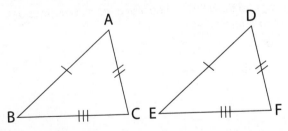

counting numbers (*números naturals*) The set of numbers used for counting (1, 2, 3,…).

cube (*un cubo*) A rectangular prism with six square sides equal in size and shape.

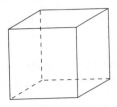

cup (*una taza*) A unit of volume in the customary measurement system, abbreviated as "c". One cup equals 8 fluid ounces.

currency symbols (*los símbolos de moneda*) Symbols used to label amounts of money. In the United States, the symbol $ represents dollars and the symbol ¢ represents cents.

customary measurement system (*el sistema de medición acostumbrada*) The system of measurement used in the United States.

customary units of measure (*las unidades de la medición acostumbradas*) The units used to measure length or distance, volume, and weight in the United States. The basic units include the foot, cup, and pound.

cylinder (*un cilindro*) A solid with two equal and parallel circular bases.

D

data (*los datos*) Information about a situation, group, or event.

day (*un día*) A twenty-four hour period starting at 12:00 midnight and ending the following midnight.

decagon (*un decágono*) A 10-sided polygon.

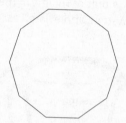

decimal fraction (*una fracción decimal*) A fraction with a power of ten (10, 100, 1,000, etc.) as the denominator. For example, 0.06 can be written as $\frac{6}{100}$. This is a decimal fraction because the denominator 100 is a power of 10.

decimal number (*un número decimal*) A number containing a decimal point. For example, 0.25 is a decimal number read as twenty-five hundredths.

decimal point (*una coma decimal*) The point in a decimal number which separates the whole numbers (to the left of the point) and the decimal fractions (to the right of the point). For example, the number 24.55 represents 24 whole units and fifty-five hundredths of another unit.

decimeter (*el decímetro*) A unit of length in the metric system, abbreviated as "dm". There are 10 decimeters in 1 meter.

degree measure of an angle (*una medida del grado de un ángulo*) A measure of the size of an angle. A circle or one complete turn measures 360°.

denominator (*un denominador*) The number below the division line in a fraction. It represents the number of equal parts into which the whole or group is divided. For example, in the fraction $\frac{3}{5}$, the denominator is 5.

difference (*la diferencia*) The result of subtracting two numbers.

digit (*un dígito*) Any of the numerals 0 to 9.

digital clock (*un reloj digital*) A timepiece that shows time without hour and minute hands.

divide (*divider*) To break a whole into parts.

dividend (*un dividendo*) The total amount you are dividing. In the example, $6 \div 3 = 2$, 6 is the dividend.

divisible (*divisible*) A number is divisible by another number when the division leaves a remainder of zero.

division (*division*) An operation that divides a whole or set into equal parts. It is performed on two numbers to get a third number called the *quotient*.

divisor (*un divisor*) The amount by which you are dividing. In the example $8 \div 4 = 2$, 4 is the divisor.

dollar (*el dólar*) The basic unit of paper money used in the United States. One dollar is equal to 100 pennies.

double (*duplicar*) To multiply by two.

E

edge (*el borde*) The line along which two sides of a solid figure meet.

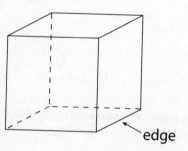
edge

elapsed time (*el tiempo transcurrido*) The amount of time that passes between the beginning and end of an event.

endpoint (*el término*) The starting or ending point of a line segment.

equal (*igual a*) Two numbers or expressions are equal if they have the same value. For example, $3 + 2 = 4 + 1$.

equation (*una ecuación*) A math sentence that uses an equal sign to show that two quantities have the same value.

equilateral triangle (*un triángulo equilateral*) A triangle with three equal sides and three equal angles. Each of the angles in an equilateral triangle measures 60°.

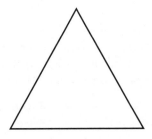

equivalent (*equivalente*) Two numbers or expressions are equivalent if they have the same value. For example, $6 + 6$ and $10 + 2$ are equivalent because both are equal to 12.

equivalent decimals (*unos decimales equivalents*) Two decimals are equivalent if they have the same value. For example, 0.2 and 0.20 are equivalent because when written as fractions, $\frac{2}{10}$ and $\frac{20}{100}$, they can both be simplified to $\frac{1}{5}$ and therefore are equal in value.

equivalent fractions (*unas fracciones equivalents*) Fractions that, when simplified to lowest terms, are exactly equal to one another. For example, $\frac{2}{4}$ and $\frac{8}{16}$ are equivalent fractions because both simplify to $\frac{1}{2}$.

equivalent numerical expressions (*unas expresiones numéricas equivalents*) Two numbers or expressions are equivalent if they have the same value. For example, 2×2 and $3 + 1$ are equivalent numerical expressions because $2 \times 2 = 4$ and $3 + 1 = 4$.

estimate (*estimar*) A result close to the exact result, found by approximating or rounding the numbers given in the problem.

estimation strategies (*estrategias de estimar*) Methods used to arrive at an approximate answer to a problem. For example, rounding numbers is one way to estimate the answer to a problem.

evaluate (*evaluar*) To use the order of operations to determine the value of an expression. For example, you can evaluate the expression $(5 + 3) \times 2$ by following the order of operations to get $8 \times 2 = 16$.

even number (*un número par*) A number that is divisible by 2. Even numbers end in 0, 2, 4, 6, or 8.

event (*el evento*) An action performed during a probability experiment. For example, rolling a die and tossing a coin are examples of events in a probability experiment.

expanded form (*la forma extendida*) The expanded form of a number shows the parts of that number broken down by place value. For example, the expanded form of 3,425 is $3,000 + 400 + 20 + 5$.

experimental results (*los resultados experimentales*) The recorded outcomes of an experiment in which a test is performed on one or more groups of subjects.

extend a pattern (*continuar una configuración*) To continue a given sequence or design by using the rule established in it. For example, the extension of the sequence 2, 4, 6, 8 is 10, 12, 14, 16.

F

face (*la cara*) A flat side of a solid figure.

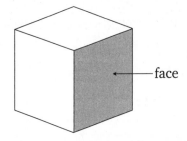

factor (noun) (*un factor*) Any of two or more quantities that are multiplied together. In the number sentence $3 \times 11 = 33$, the factors are 3 and 11.

APPENDICES

factor (verb) (*descomponer en factores*) To write a number or expression as a product of its factors. For example, 14 can be factored as 2×7.

fifths (*quintos*) One or more of five equal parts of a whole.

foot (*un pie*) A unit of length in the customary measurement system, abbreviated as "ft". One foot equals 12 inches.

formula (*una formula*) A rule that describes how to calculate a certain quantity or measurement. For example, the formula for the area of a rectangle is $A = l \times w$, where A represents the area, l represents the length, and w represents the width.

formulate conclusions from graphs (*hacer conclusiones de una gráfica*) To summarize information from the data shown in a graph.

formulate predictions from graphs (*hacer predicciones de una gráfica*) To guess or estimate future data by extending a pattern shown in a graph.

four-digit number (*un número de cuatro dígitos*) A number containing 4 numerals, each of which can range from 0–9. For example, 2,367 is a four-digit number.

fourths (*los cuartos*) One or more of four equal parts of a whole.

fraction (*una fracción*) A number in the form $\frac{\text{numerator}}{\text{denominator}}$, where the numerator and denominator are whole numbers and the denominator is not zero.

Fractions are used to represent parts of a whole object or part of a collection of objects. For example, $\frac{1}{3}$ is a fraction that represents one out of three equal parts of a whole.

frequency table (*un cuadro de frecuencias*) A table which summarizes the number of times a value or event occurred.

front-end estimation (*la estimación frontal*) A way of estimating the solution to a problem by rounding each number to its largest place value and then mentally calculating the answer. For example, to mentally estimate 6,432 + 2,297, round the numbers to 6,000 + 2,000 to get 8,000.

G

gallon (*un galón*) A unit of volume in the customary measurement system, abbreviated as "gal". A gallon is equal to 4 quarts.

geometric figure (*una figura geométrica*) Any shape consisting of a set of points. For example, a line, line segment, plane, triangle, rectangle, cube, and sphere are all geometric figures.

geometric pattern (*una configuración geométrica*) A design created using shapes (such as lines, squares, circles, triangles, and rectangles).

geometry (*la geometría*) The study of points, lines, angles, planes, shapes, and solids.

gram (*un gramo*) The basic unit of weight in the metric system, abbreviated as "g".

greater than (*más de*) A number is greater than another number if its value is larger. For example, 200 > 150 because 200 has a larger value than 150.

greatest common divisor, GCD (*el máximo divisor en común*) The largest number that divides evenly into two or more other numbers. For example, the greatest common divisor of 18 and 27 is 9. (Also known as the greatest common factor.)

greatest common factor, GCF (*el máximo factor en común*) The largest number that is a factor of two or more numbers. For example, the greatest common factor of 18 and 27 is 9. (Also known as the greatest common divisor.)

H

half hour (*media hora*) A unit of time equal to 30 minutes.

halves (*las mitades*) One of two equal parts of a whole.

halving (*partir en dos*) To divide a number, object, or group of objects into two equal parts.

heptagon (*un heptágono*) A seven-sided polygon.

hexagon (*un hexágono*) A six-sided polygon.

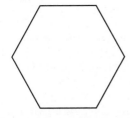

hour (*la hora*) A unit of time equal to 60 minutes.

hundred chart (*un cuadro de gráficos de cien*) A 10 × 10 table labeled 1 through 100 used to learn counting to 100, skip counting, and number patterns.

hundred thousands (*cien miles*) Any of the first nine multiples of the number 100,000.

hundreds (*cientos/as*) Any of the first nine multiples of the number 100.

hundreds place (*el valor posicional de los cien*) A place value in the base-ten number system that represents the number of 100s that are in a number. It is located three places to the left of the decimal point.

hundredths (*centésimo*) A place value in the base-ten number system representing a number of $\frac{1}{100}$ s that are in a number. It is located two places to the right of the decimal point.

I

identity element for multiplication (*el elemento de identidad para la multiplicación*) The number 1, because no matter what number it is multiplied by, it always results in that number. For example, $1 \times 7 = 7$.

impossible outcomes (*resultados imposibles*) Outcomes of an experiment that cannot happen. For example, when testing probability by rolling a six-sided number cube labeled 1 through 6, rolling a 7 is an impossible outcome.

improper fraction (*una fracción impropia*) A fraction in which the numerator is larger than the denominator and the denominator is not zero. For example, $\frac{6}{5}$ is an improper fraction.

inch (*una pulgada*) A unit of length in the customary measurement system, abbreviated as "in." Twelve inches equal one foot.

inequality (*una inecuación*) A math sentence that uses symbols such as > (greater than) and < (less than) to compare values. For example, $10 > 7$ is an inequality.

input values (*el valor puesto*) An input value is a number that is put into a number sentence to produce another number (output value). For example, the input value 4 can be put into the number sentence $m = n + 2$ for n to get $m = 4 + 2$. Therefore, $m = 6$ is the output value.

interior angles (*unos ángulos interiores*) Angles on the inside of a polygon formed by two connecting sides of the polygon.

intersecting lines (*lineas que se crucen*) Two lines that intersect at a point.

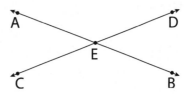

inverse operations (*las operaciones inversas*) Operations that are opposites. Addition is the inverse operation of subtraction, and multiplication is the inverse operation of division.

APPENDICES

inverse property of addition (*la propiedad inversa de adición*) The sum of a number and its opposite is zero. For example, $5 + (-5) = 0$.

inverse property of multiplication (*la propiedad inversa de multiplicación*) The product of a number and its reciprocal is 1. For example, the reciprocal of 3 is $\frac{1}{3}$. Therefore $3 \times \frac{1}{3} = 1$.

irregular polygon (*un polígono irregular*) A polygon that does not have equal sides and equal angles.

isosceles triangle (*un triángulo isósceles*) A triangle with exactly two equal sides and two equal angles.

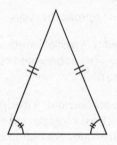

K

key to a graph (*la clave de una gráfica*) A small area near a graph which explains the meanings of the symbols or markings on that graph.

kilogram (*el kilogramo*) A unit of mass in the metric system, abbreviated as "kg". One kilogram equals 1,000 grams.

kilometer (*el kilómetro*) A unit of length in the metric system, abbreviated as "km". One kilometer equals 1,000 meters.

L

least common denominator, LCD (*el denominador común más bajo*) The smallest number that is a multiple of the denominators of 2 or more fractions. For example, the least common denominator of $\frac{3}{4}$ and $\frac{1}{6}$ is 12 because 12 is the smallest number that is a multiple of both 4 and 6.

least common multiple, LCM (*el múltiplo común más bajo*) The smallest number that is a multiple of two or more numbers. For example, the least common multiple of 6 and 8 is 24.

length (*la longitud*) The distance across a line segment or a side of a polygon.

less than (*menos de*) A number is less than another number if its value is smaller. For example, $85 < 99$ because 85 has a smaller value than 99.

like denominators (*los denominadores communes*) Two or more denominators that are the same. For example, $\frac{4}{9}$ and $\frac{8}{9}$ share a like denominator, which is 9. (Also known as "the common denominator.")

line (*una línea*) An infinite set of points that forms a straight path with no endpoints.

line graph (*una gráfica de línea*) A graph that uses lines or line segments to indicate relationships among data.

line of symmetry (*la línea de simetría*) A line of symmetry divides a figure so that when the image is folded along the line, the two sides match exactly.

line segment (*un segmento de una línea*) A set of points that forms a straight path with two endpoints.

liter (*el litro*) The basic unit of volume in the metric system, abbreviated (L).

lowest terms (*los términos más bajos*) When the numerator and denominator of a fraction have no factors greater than 1 in common. For example, $\frac{8}{12}$ written in lowest terms is $\frac{2}{3}$ because both the numerator and denominator can be divided by 4. The fraction $\frac{3}{8}$ is already in lowest terms. (Also known as "simplest form.")

M

mass (*la masa*) The amount of matter that an object contains.

mean (*la media aritmética*) The average of a set of numbers. The mean is found by dividing the sum of the set by the number of pieces in it. For example, the mean of {3, 4, 5} is found by adding 3 + 4 + 5 to get 12, and then dividing 12 by 3 (the amount of numbers added together) to get 4.

measure (*medir*) To obtain the quantity, length, weight, or volume of an object (or set of objects) or liquid.

measurement (*una medida*) The quantity, length, weight, or volume of an object (or set of objects) or liquid.

mental math (*el cálculo mental*) A calculation done without pencil, paper, calculator, or computer.

meter (*un metro*) A unit of length in the metric system, abbreviated as "m". One meter equals 100 centimeters.

metric system (*el sistema métrico*) A system of measurement that is based on units of 10.

metric units of measure (*las unidades de medida métricas*) The units of measure based on units of 10. The basic units of the metric system are the meter, liter, and gram.

mile (*una milla*) A unit of distance in the customary measurement system. One mile equals 5,280 feet.

milliliter (*un mililitro*) A unit of volume in the metric system, abbreviated as "mL". One liter equals 1,000 milliliters.

millimeter (*un milímetro*) A unit of length in the metric system, abbreviated as "mm". One meter equals 1,000 millimeters.

millions (*los millones*) Any of the first nine multiples of the number 1,000,000, which equals 1,000 × 1,000.

minute (*un minuto*) A unit of time equal to 60 seconds. There are 60 minutes in one hour.

mixed number (*un número mixto*) A number that is comprised of a whole number and a fraction. For example, $4\frac{1}{2}$ is a mixed number.

multiple (*un múltiplo*) The product of a given integer and a counting number. For example, the number 3 has multiples such as 3, 6, 9, 12, 15, 18, etc.

multiplicand (*un multiplicando*) The number being multiplied in a multiplication problem.

multiplication (*multiplicación*) An operation on two numbers, called *factors*, to obtain a third number called the *product*. For example, 4 × 6 yields 24.

multiplier (*un multiplicador*) The number by which another number is multiplied in a multiplication problem.

multiply (*multiplicar*) To perform an operation on two numbers, called *factors*, to obtain a third number, called the *product*. For example, to multiply two numbers such as 7 and 3, you write 7 × 3 = 21.

N

nonagon (*un nonágono*) A nine-sided polygon.

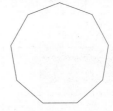

nonstandard measure (*una medida no estándar*) A measurement found using unusual units of measure such as paper clips, sticks of gum, shoes, etc.

not equal to (*desigual a*) Two numbers or expressions are not equal to each other if they do not have the same value. For example 3 ≠ 5 means 3 is not equal to 5.

number (*un número*) A digit or series of digits representing a certain numeric value.

number line (*la línea de números*) A line on which points are marked off at regular intervals (i.e., evenly spaced) and labeled with ordered numbers.

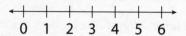

number sentence (*una frase de números*)

A true numeric statement containing numbers, operation symbols, and either $>$, $<$, $\geq$, $\leq$, $\neq$, or $=$. It can also contain variables. For example, $3 + 6 = 9$, $7 > 1 + 3$, or $\frac{3}{5} + \frac{1}{5} = \frac{4}{5}$.

number system (*el sistema de numeración*) A way of representing and counting numbers. For example, the decimal system represents numbers using a decimal point and place values such as ones, tens, and hundreds.

numeral (*el numeral*) Any digit from 0–9.

numeration (*la numeración*) The counting of numbers.

numerator (*un numerador*) The number above the division line in a fraction. It represents the number of equal parts being described. For example, in the fraction $\frac{3}{5}$, 3 is the numerator and it represents three out of five equal parts.

numeric expression (*una expresión numérica*)
A math phrase that contains numbers and operation symbols, but no variables or relation systems. For example, $3 \times 6 + 9$ is a numeric expression.

numeric patterns (*unas configuraciones numéricas*) A repeating rule in a group of numbers. For example, in the group of numbers 4, 8, 12, 16, 20, the pattern is "add 4."

numerical problems (*unos problemas numéricos*) A math problem that contains numbers and operation symbols.

numerically (*numéricamente*) A problem is expressed numerically if it contains numbers and operation symbols such as $+$, $-$, $\div$, $\times$.

obtuse angle (*el ángulo obtuso*) An angle whose measure is between 90° and 180°.

obtuse triangle (*el triángulo obtuso*) A triangle with one angle greater than 90°.

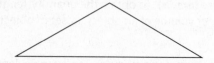

octagon (*el octágono*) An eight-sided polygon.

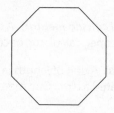

odd number (*los números impares*) An integer that ends in 1, 3, 5, 7, or 9.

ones (*unos*) One represents an individual unit equal in value to the number 1.

ones place (*el valor posicional de uno*) A place value in the base-ten number system that represents the number of 1s that are in a number. It is located one place to the left of the decimal point.

open figure (*una figura abierta*) A figure in which the beginning and end points do not touch.

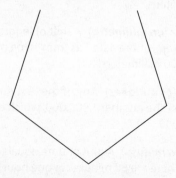

open sentence (*una frase numérica abierta*)
A number sentence containing one or more variables. For example, $x + 6 = 8$.

operation (*la operación*) A process performed on numbers. The basic operations are addition, subtraction, multiplication, and division.

order (*ordenar*) To put in a sequence from least to greatest or from greatest to least.

order of operations (*el orden de operaciones*) A rule indicating the order in which operations should be performed in an expression. Perform operations inside parentheses first, then simplify exponents. Next, perform multiplication and division from left to right, and finally perform addition and subtraction from left to right.

organized chart (*una carta organizada*) A chart used to put information into categories using rows and columns.

organized list (*una lista organizada*) A list of numbers or other information arranged in categories or columns.

ounce (*una onza*) A unit of weight in the customary measurement system, abbreviated as "oz". There are 16 ounces in one pound. It can also refer to a unit of volume. Eight fluid ounces equal one cup.

P

parallel lines (*las líneas paralelas*) Two different lines in the same plane which never intersect.

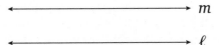

parallelogram (*el paralelogramo*) A four-sided polygon with opposite sides parallel and equal.

part (*la parte*) A section of a whole.

pattern (*una configuración*) Regularity found in nature, a situation, an event, a design, or a set of numbers (e.g., spirals on pineapples, designs in quilts, the number sequence 3, 6, 9, 12,…).

pentagon (*un pentágono*) A five-sided polygon.

percent (*por ciento*) A ratio which compares a number to 100. The symbol for percent is %. For example, 50% means 50 out of 100, and 35% means 35 out of 100.

perimeter (*el perímetro*) The distance around a polygon. This distance can be found by adding the lengths of the sides.

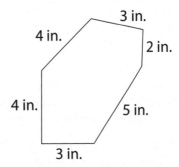

perimeter = 21 in.

perpendicular lines (*unas líneas perpendiculares*) Lines that intersect to form right angles.

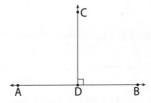

personal references (*unas referencias personales*) The use of personal measurements, such as arm length or hand length to measure an object. For example, a hand is approximately 6 inches. Therefore, if a desk is 7 hands long then it is $7 \times 6 = 42$ inches long.

pictograph (*un pictograma*) A graph in which pictures are used to represent values.

pint (*una pinta*) A measure of volume, abbreviated as "pt". Two cups equal 1 pint; 2 pints equal 1 quart.

place value (*el valor posicional*) The value of a digit depending on its position in a number. In the numeral 5,270, the 2 is in the hundreds place, which gives it a value of 200.

plane figure (*una figura plana*) A figure that lies in only one plane. Circles, squares, rectangles, and parallelograms are examples of plane figures.

plot (*trazar*) To graph ordered pairs (x, y) on the coordinate plane.

point (*el punto*) A location in space represented by a dot. The point is the basis for building all other figures such as line segments, circles, squares, etc.

poll (*una encuesta*) To ask a group of people the same question or set of questions to organize and analyze the answers.

polygon (*un polígono*) A figure with three or more sides in which each side is a line segment. For example, squares, rectangles, parallelograms, and trapezoids are polygons.

possible outcomes (*unos resultados posibles*) The possible results of an experiment. For example, when rolling a six-sided number cube, the possible outcomes are 1, 2, 3, 4, 5, and 6.

post meridian, P.M. (*después del mediodía*) The label given to the hours between 12:00 noon and 12:00 midnight.

pound (*una libra*) A unit of weight in the customary measurement system, abbreviated as "lb". One pound equals 16 ounces. Two thousand pounds equal one ton.

prediction (*una predicción*) An educated guess about the outcome of an event or several events. For example, when tossing a coin 10 times, a prediction could be that the coin will land on heads 5 times.

prime number (*un número primo*) A whole number greater than one that has only two factors: 1 and itself. For example, 2, 3, 5, 7, and 11 are prime numbers.

prism (*una prisma*) A solid formed by four or more flat sides that intersect with bases. For example, a rectangular prism is shown below.

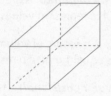

probability (*la probabilidad*) The likelihood or chance of an event occurring, expressed as a number from 0 to 1. A probability of 1 means that the event is certain to occur, while a probability of 0 means that the event cannot occur.

product (*el producto*) The solution to a multiplication problem. For example, in the number sentence $3 \times 5 = 15$, the product is 15.

proper fraction (*una fracción propia*) A fraction in which the numerator is smaller than the denominator. For example, $\frac{5}{8}$ is a proper fraction.

property (*la propiedad*) A rule used to simplify expressions. For example, the commutative property states that the order in which numbers are added does not change the sum: $4 + 2 = 2 + 4$.

protractor (*un transportador*) A tool used to measure angles in degrees.

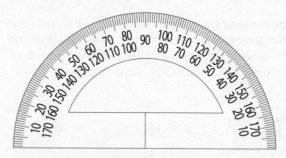

pyramid (*un pirámide*) A solid with a polygon as a base and triangles for faces that meet at a point on top.

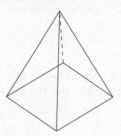

Q

quadrant (*un cuadrante*) One of the four sections of a coordinate plane.

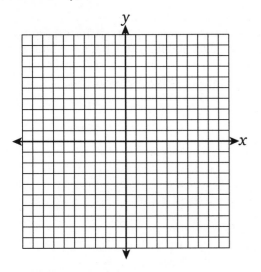

quadrilateral (*un cuadrilátero*) A four-sided polygon.

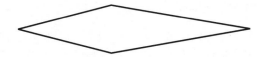

quart (*un cuarto*) A unit of liquid measure, abbreviated as "qt". Two pints equal one quart, and 4 quarts equal 1 gallon.

quotient (*un cociente*) The answer when dividing a number by another number. For example, in the number sentence $6 \div 3 = 2$, the quotient is 2.

R

ratio (*una proporción*) A comparison of two numbers, often written as a fraction. For example, if there are three boys in class for every two girls, the ratio of boys to girls is $\frac{3}{2}$ or 3:2 (read as "3 to 2").

ray (*un rayo*) A part of a line that extends from a given point in one direction only.

reasonable estimate (*unas estimaciones razonables*) A guess at an answer that is within the range of possible answers.

rectangle (*el rectángulo*) A four-sided polygon with opposite sides parallel and four right angles.

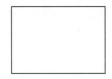

regroup (*reagrupar*) To reorganize the values in a number to carry out addition and subtraction.

Subtraction with regrouping:

$$\begin{array}{r} \overset{3\ 10}{7\cancel{4}\cancel{0}} \\ -519 \\ \hline 221 \end{array}$$

regular polygon (*un polígono regular*) A polygon with equal sides and equal angles. For example, a square is a regular polygon because all of its sides are equal and all of its angles are equal.

related facts (*los hechos relacionados*) Information that is needed to solve a problem.

remainder (*el resto*) A whole number that is left over after one whole number is divided by another. For example, when dividing 8 by 6, the answer is 1 with a remainder of 2.

rhombus (*un rombo*) A four-sided polygon with opposite sides parallel and four equal sides.

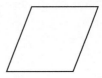

right angle (*un ángulo recto*) An angle that measures exactly 90°.

rounding (*redondear un número*) An action that changes a number to a more convenient value. For example, to round to the nearest hundred, find the hundred that is closest to the given number; that is, 4,295 rounded to the nearest hundred is 4,300.

APPENDICES

rule (*una regla*) A sequence of steps that can be used to solve a problem or perform an action on a number.

ruler (*una regla*) A tool used to measure the length of objects in inches or in centimeters.

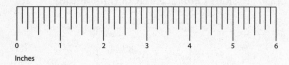

Inches

S

sample space (*las posibilidades*) The set of all possible outcomes of an experiment.

scale on a graph (*la escala de una gráfica*) The labeled numbers that increase by equal amounts on the *x*- and *y*-axes.

scale to measure mass (*la balanza*) A tool used to determine the weight of an object.

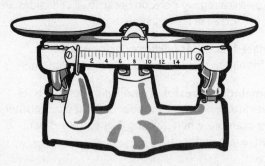

scalene triangle (*un triángulo escaleno*) A triangle that does not have any equal sides or angles.

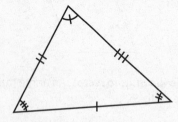

second (*un segundo*) A unit of time. Sixty seconds equal one minute.

set of data (*un colección de datos*) A collection of numbers or information about objects or events.

set of objects (*un colección de objetos*) A collection of shapes or entities.

shape (*una figura*) A closed figure in space. Squares, circles, triangles, rhombi, and rectangles are all examples of shapes.

side (*un lado*) One of the line segments that make up a polygon.

similar figures (*unas figuras similares*) Figures that have the same shape but not necessarily the same size. All corresponding angles are equal, and all corresponding sides are proportional.

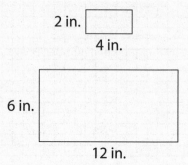

similar triangles (*unos triángulos similares*) Triangles that have the same shape but not necessarily the same size.

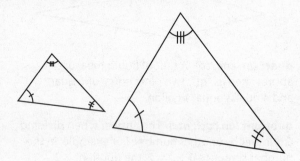

simplest form (*los términos más bajos*) When the numerator and denominator have no factors greater than 1 in common. For example, $\frac{8}{12}$ written in simplest form is $\frac{2}{3}$ because both numerator and denominator can be divided by 4. The fraction $\frac{3}{8}$ is already in simplest form. (Also known as "lowest terms.")

simplify fractions (*simplificar fracciones*) To write a fraction in simplest form.

single event (*un evento singular*) One of a set of tests performed during a probability experiment.

single-event experiment (*un experimiento de un evento singular*) An experiment whose outcome is determined by one occurrence or event. For example, a single-event experiment could involve tossing a coin once.

sixths (*los sextos*) One or more of six equal parts of a whole.

skip-count (*contar saltando unos numeros*) Counting by multiples of a number. For example, skip-counting by 2s gives the sequence 2, 4, 6, 8,... and skip-counting by 5s gives the sequence 5, 10, 15, 20,....

solid figure (*una figura sólida*) A three-dimensional figure with length, depth, and height, such as a cube, cylinder, or pyramid.

solve (*solucionar*) To determine the answer to a problem.

sphere (*una esfera*) The set of all points in a space that are the same distance from a given point in that space, called the *center*.

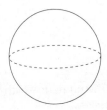

square (*un cuadro*) A four-sided polygon with four equal sides and four equal angles.

standard measure (*las unidades de la medida estándar*) The customary units of measure used in the United States. The basic units include the foot, cup, and pound.

straight angle (*un ángulo recto*) An angle with a measure of exactly 180°.

substitute (*sustituir*) To replace an unknown in a number sentence with a number of equal value.

subtract (*sustraer*) To take away one number from another. To subtract, the sign "−" is used. For example, 6 − 4 = 2.

subtraction (*sustracción*) The process of taking away a number from another number. To subtract, the sign "−" is used. For example, 6 − 4 = 2.

sum (*la suma*) The result of adding two or more numbers.

survey (*una encuesta*) An interview of a group to find information such as likes, dislikes, needs, and wants.

symbols in verbal form (*los símbolos en forma verbal*) Ways of representing numbers and objects that are written on paper or spoken in words. For example, the expression "*m* + 7" means "7 more than *m*."

symbols in written form (*los símbolos en forma escrita*) Ways of representing numbers and objects on paper without using numbers. For example, a variable such as *n* is an example of a symbol that can be written to represent an unknown number.

T

table (*una tabla*) A display of information organized into rows and columns so that the facts can be easily read or understood.

ten thousands (*diez milésimos*) Any of the first nine multiples of 10,000.

tens (*decenas*) Any of the first nine multiples of the number 10.

tens place (*el valor posicional de los diez*) A place value in the base-ten number system that represents the number of 10s that are in a number. It is located two places to the left of the decimal point.

tenths (*décimos*) One or more of ten equal parts of a whole.

thirds (*terceros*) One or more of three equal parts of a whole.

thousands (*miles*) Any of the first nine multiples of the number 1,000.

thousandths (*millares*) One or more of the number $\frac{1}{1,000}$.

three-digit number (*un número tridigital*) A number containing 3 numerals, each of which can range from 0–9. For example, 455 is a three-digit number.

three-dimensional figure (*una figura tridimensional*) A figure in space that has a height, width, and depth.

time (*el tiempo*) A system of keeping track of the minutes and hours in a day. There are 24 hours in one day and 60 minutes in each hour.

ton (*una tonelada*) A unit of weight in the customary measurement system. One ton equals 2,000 pounds.

translate (*trasladar*) To move a figure to a new position without turning or flipping the figure.

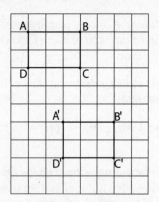

trapezoid (*un trapezoide*) A four-sided polygon with exactly one pair of parallel sides.

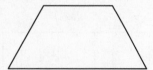

triangle (*el triángulo*) A three-sided polygon. The sum of the interior angles of a triangle is 180°.

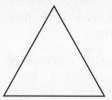

two-dimensional figure (*una figura de dos dimensiones*) A figure in a plane which has a height and a width.

U

unit fraction (*una fracción unitaria*) A fraction with 1 as the numerator and any integer as the denominator. For example, $\frac{1}{4}$ is a unit fraction.

unlike denominators (*unos denominadores desemejantes*) Denominators of two or more fractions that are not the same. For example, $\frac{2}{5}$ and $\frac{7}{8}$ have unlike denominators, namely 5 and 8.

V

value (*el valor*) The numeric worth of a digit, variable, or expression.

variable (*una variable*) An unknown quantity. A variable may be represented by a letter.

verbal expression (*una expresión verbal*) A combination of numbers, variables, and operations written or spoken in words. For example, "James found 3 more than 2 times as many seashells as Jorge."

vertex (*el vértice*) The point shared by two rays or line segments forming an angle. It can also refer to the point at which two lines intersect. It can also refer to the point at which three faces of a rectangular prism meet.

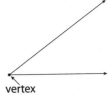

vertex

vertices (*los vértices*) The plural of *vertex*.

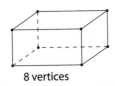

8 vertices

W

week (*la semana*) A unit of time equal to 7 days.

whole (*entero*) The sum of all the parts of a number or object.

whole number (*un número entero*) Any of the set of numbers {0, 1, 2, 3, 4,…}.

whole unit (*una unidad entera*) A number or object not divided into parts.

Y

yard (*una yarda*) A unit of length in the customary measurement system, abbreviated as "yd". One yard is equal to three feet.

Z

zero property of addition (*la propiedad de cero de adición*) The sum of 0 and any number is that number. For example, $0 + 5 = 5$.

zero property of multiplication (*la propiedad de cero de multiplicación*) When multiplying any number by 0, the answer is 0. For example, $9 \times 0 = 0$.